Friends With You

Tiny friends, larger than life by Sonja Commentz

Time to enter a land of fairy tales where the boundaries between fact and fiction blur – and nobody could care less.

Samuel Borkson and Arturo (Tury) Sandoval aka FriendsWithYou are two men with a mission and vision: to make art universally accessible and carry some of the pure and unadulterated joy of childhood into our adult realm.
Born with "an instinct to create, skills in papier mache, fruit baskets and now video, motion graphics, microbe taming and breeding," the Miami-based design collective have been spreading their visual philosophy since 2002.

It all started out in the tangible realm, with hand-stitched custom patterns for their first line of magical plush toy arts. What began as a small sideline project soon developed a life of its own: reminiscent of long lost childhood friends, their evocative toys and characters proved an instant hit with kids and grown-ups alike – immensely and instantly loveable, these little critters appeal to and embody our basic pre-pubescent instincts: protection, hunger, security, friendship, escape and a glowingly childish view of the world.
With backgrounds in fine art and advertising, FWY were well aware of the power of brands and seduction. "Looking at the world through advertising eyes gives you an entirely new perspective on art in today's world. Every day we compete with an immeasurable amount of conscious or subconscious memory signals. Once we have attracted people's attention with something as visually powerful as the Malfi (their trademark character), they are drawn into out world, eager to find out more."
Iconic by nature, FWY's characters rely on their creators' perfect command of visual language, paring sensations down to their bare essentials. "This is something everyone can relate to immediately, it's the square root of conveying a feeling. It's about archetypes and icons, the main ingredients that make and break all cultures. We were the first people raised by icons; we know Batman, Pacman and Mickey better than any scientist or Nobel Prize winner. Our heroes are all fantasy and they are so much better than the human qualities they represent."
Luck, for example, comes in all shapes and guises. Literally. Storytellers par excellence, FWY imbue each of their creations with a magical history and equally magic powers, turning them into something akin to voodoo dolls and avatars for modern society. Amid their weird and wonderful rabble of 'Friends', imaginary microbes blown-up to user-friendly sizes and equipped with "actual life-enhancing skills", we have King Albino, who will happily erase all of life's embarrassing moments, Black Foot to open and close all doors, Berry to soften the blows of mental and physical ailments plus myriads of other tiny helpers to provide comfort, aid us in decision-making or simply whisk us away to another world. And, lest we forget, "Albino Squid is a jerk. He is a useful friend in that he reminds you how not to act."
A temporary respite from mundane reality, FWY invite us to join their own adventure-soaked universe – and share our wishes and desires with these newly acquired friends.

Imbued with these characteristics, their characters provide an exact indication of what we are - or wish we were. Simple, fun and innocent as they might seem, they also serve as a mirror and extension of their creators – and human nature itself. "For anybody who connects with them, it means that they feel it reflects something they love about themselves. It is our job, as creative people, to observe the good and evil of the world and make sure we understand that we are a bit of both. We believe that this is the most human form of art and that is why it will change the world. So get a little dirty, believe in magic, luck and friendship, and help us to spread it."

Enchanted messengers of their creed, FWY's wild array of endearing friends tend to shift, change and reincarnate with the times, tides and new discoveries. Skirting the boundaries between covetable toy, art and quasi-religious artefact, their ecosphere keeps evolving and mutating, occasionally even spilling over into earthly realms as interactive wishing wells or larger-than-life surreal playgrounds. Thus moving beyond playful art for desk, shelf or bedside table, FWY sneak more and more of their little helpers into our everyday lives – from sketches and paintings via toys and films to hotel rooms and public art installations.
An impressive breadth, yet to Sam and Tury, the choice of medium is simply an immensely fun means to an end, a beautiful vehicle for their universal message of friendship, enlightenment and creativity. United in their benign mission to become Friends With You, their projects favour simplicity as a blank slate for their ever-changing

dream worlds, teeming with recurring permutations of basic shapes and characters. Crystalline structures, rainbows galore, and a hint of op-art herald a long-overdue return to an almost psychedelic, colourful and joyful realm of ur-symbols, a primordial soup of creation with a very contemporary touch.

Nevertheless, their ultimate goal transcends this visual wonderland. Akin to a secret society, made up of all who endorse the FWY spirit, Sam and Tury have set their sights on a higher aim: "In the sterile settings of modern society, spiritual outlets have become low priority within our daily routines. Replaced by capitalist ideals, rigid religious requirements and other self-centred activities, our daily lives are rarely touched by anything void of monetary value."
With their colourful creations FWY aim to fill this spiritual hole and establish a new sense of perception, a movement, an encompassing 'friendship' based on participation and interaction. Both artists are well aware that phrases like 'mission', 'spreading the word' or 'movement' are likely to trigger alarm bells, fine-tuned to any kind of cultish overtones. Sam and Tury's universe, however, has no rules or commandments, no forsworn beliefs. "All we want to convey is magic, luck and friendship. I guess you could see it as a club that accepts people from all religions and cultures – each person, animal, even each blade of grass is already a part of it. We are all Friends With You."
Pre-rational and anti-materialist by nature, suffused by their honest conviction and boundless enthusiasm, this disarming naivety and complete lack of distancing irony may be unsettling at first – it is something we are simply not used to any more. And yet, for those who dare to take the plunge, FWY's encompassing, tailor-made wonderland offers a beautiful, temporary respite from all things pragmatic, infused with a rare sense of joy and wonder.

But what would a world be without its creator(s)? Much of what shapes the ever-expanding FWY empire is born of the relationship between its two human nuclei: "We work together flawlessly - each one of us is strong where the other isn't. I work through the night and Tury wakes up right when I go to sleep. It is a constantly changing and amazing adventure, ultimately a stream of magical occurrences and instances. Our combined energies create something truly magical - even when we are working on our own projects we keep exploring the same ideas, since we both feel that this is an exercise that helps us grow our own visual and artistic language." A truly symbiotic relationship and visible proof that friendship can spur us on to greater heights - "the amount of time and power we put into these projects is directly transferred to the people who experience it."

From magic realism to real magic, childlike, but never infantile, FWY's tightly woven realm effortlessly bridges the gap between toy culture and art, taking those who steer clear of museums that decisive step closer. Tirelessly chipping away at the fabric of our perceived reality to supply us with an endless stream of hugely inventive and covetable reminders of what it is like to enjoy and believe, FWY have created something very rare: art and spirituality you can touch – and that touches you in return.
Rain or shine – prepare for sublime enchantment!

THE BURGERBUNCH
Friends With You

Plush Toys

MALFI - Malfi will bring you great wealth or death. Good luck and be careful.

MR. TTT - ONE of our most amazing achievements was the induction of this luck friend. We all know the best things come in threes, especially LUCK! Like to share? Mr.TTT splits into 3 PARTS! Make new friends today without giving him all away. We have found that a shared Mr. TTT is three times as lucky as rabbits feet and golden horseshoes.

BARBY with SPIRIT SUIT - Comes with removable spirit mask. Barby is known for his shyness and modesty. He wears a mask for full focus and is in a constant state of meditation. If you need Barby to help you sort out a situation or just for a light conversation, remove his mask and Barby will give you complete love and attention.

ALBINO SQUID - Albino Squid is a jerk. He is a useful friend in that he reminds you how not to act. OR if you, yourself, are a jerk, then meet your new teammate in life. He wants to kick the asses of all your competitors and help you rule the world!

POPPINGS - Comes with detachable feet/babies. Are you ready to PARTY. Poppings is the charm and charisma you've always been wishing you had. Don't be nervous make a new friend, delight a bum, get that job. Everything will be at your fingertips with a lucky Poppings. Going on a date? Carry one of the Poppings feet in your purse or pocket for instant approval!

RED FLYER AND PESUS - Ever wondered what God looks like? Well this is him, and boy, does he look different. At the subatomic level, Red Flyer is literally the fabric of space as we understand it. He is what makes up the earth, the air, the water and, well, everything. Swipe your arm through the air and you are reconfiguring an unimaginable amount of red flyers. In his enlarged state, he offers invincibility and absolute power to his human companion.
PESUS is a small chunk of Red Flyer and is probably one of the potent parts, kind of like the best cut of meat.

BERRY CARRY & BARRY - Comes with a baby. A soft huggable friend, this fluffy pillow is actually the tiniest protein particle in existence. Use him as a gift for a distressed friend or a malnourished cousin. Berry Carry will grant you a healthy body and a healthy state of mind. Berry acts as a pillow to soften the blows of mental and physical ailments.

SHOEBACA - Comes with 2 detachable kidneys! Not to be surgically implanted into small children! except those without kidneys. Shoebaca is one of the most interesting friends in that, he can communicate telekinetically with his human companion. Shoebaca will help with the toughest decisions you are making in life. Remove his kidneys and ask away, then concentrate for the solutions to all your problems.

KING ALBINO - "Pigment stealer." King Albino GETS RID OF SKIN DISCOLORATION FOREVER! This little magic friend is the direct agent for all Albino animals, and he is also found in chemicals like bleach. From a one-night stand to a bad investment, let King Albino erase all of life's embarrassing moments, so you can move forward in life CAREFREE and HAPPY.

The Good Wood Gang

From the Black Forest comes a new type of lucky amulet. A wooden charm that dates back to the five ancient child gods, and the toys that delighted them. They can bring magic and mystery into your life. All have special powers and work in different ways for different people. If you treat them with respect, they will grant you all your wishes.
Black Foot aka Captain Bingo opens and closes all doors. Sweet Tooth brings you success and surprises. Lucky Doovoo can solve all your problems, like love, health, distress. Squid Racer, a triple team of power, unites to help you achieve your goals, and THE rare Mr. TTT BURGER will satisfy all your indulgences and help you to a delicious existence while showing you the key to immortality.

BLACK FOOT aka CAPTAIN BINGO - PLAY MY GAME! I RULE THE UNIVERSE! Try your hand at arranging your own luck. Is Black Foot tall? Is Captain Bingo small? It's up to you. Luck comes in all shapes and sizes. This lucky totem opens and closes all doors and possesses the key to all of life's ultimate adventures.

MR.TTT BURGER - Can YOU BELIEVE IT? A rare mixture of the finest ingredients, TTT Burger will satisfy all your indulgences and help you to a delicious existence while helping you enjoy the great life you have. Mr. TTT burger is the totem of Bumble Grump, the godchild of luck.

SWEET TOOTH is the sweetest! He always gets what he wants, but you have to give him what he needs, candy, a golden lock, or tiny mirrors and he'll let you in on his secrets. He represents the TRIPLETS of good fortune; Sweet Tooth is the sugar god head and will bring you surprises, Lil' Bernie represents the content child. Use this head for a stress free day. Baby Derwin has super powers and gives you the possibility to have really good luck or really bad luck. Which head will you choose today? Be Risky! GET BETTER RESULTS!

SQUID RACER - God of the Sea, Squid Racer uses the power of momentum to keep your life progressing until you reach your ultimate potential. This squid has fully evolved into one of the fastest, hardest working teams ever. Driven by the faithful Elby and navigated by Singing Robot Head, he is fully equipped and ready to help you take over the world!

LUCKY DOOVOO - Lucky Doovoo is a dream guide who is always sleeping.
Make all your dreams come true with the help of his enchanted blackboard. Make a secret drawing; write the name of someone you love. All your wishes can become reality with Lucky Doovoo on your side! He has three belly button articles you can choose, Insert the Ruby to concentrate on your goals, insert the heart to concentrate on your relationships, and insert the lollipop for carefree sleep!

The Malfis - Yellow Malfi, Super Malfi, Blue Malfi (top row) - Original Malfi, Mini Malfi, Naked Mini Malfi, Naked Malfi (bottom row)

The Burger Bunch - Muffin, the whole bunch (top row) - Bumble Grump, Mr. TTT Burger , Mr. TTT Burger details (bottom row)

Poppings & Mini Poppings, Mr. TTT with Mini-TTT's (top row) - Berry Carry & Barry, Shoebaka & Mini Shoebaka (middle row) - Red Flyer & Mini Red Flyer, Mr. TTT (bottom row)

Xuxa, The Boy (top row) - Fou Fee, Fee Fee, Treasure Whale (middle row) - The Luckies (bottom row)

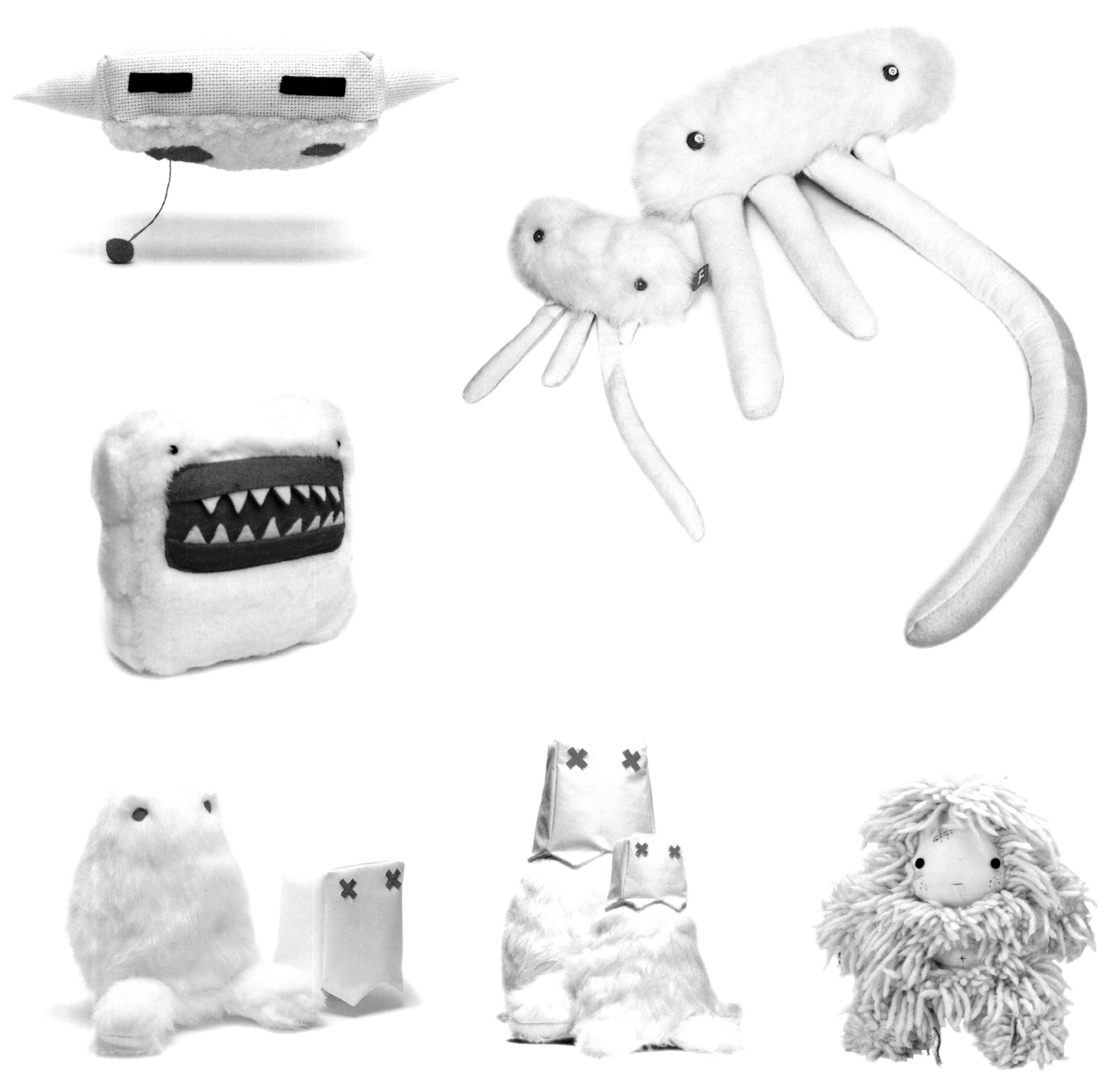

Pesus, Albino Squid (top row) - Mini King Albino (middle row) - Barby & Mini Barby with Spirit Suit off / on, Herbert (bottom row)

2L1 4

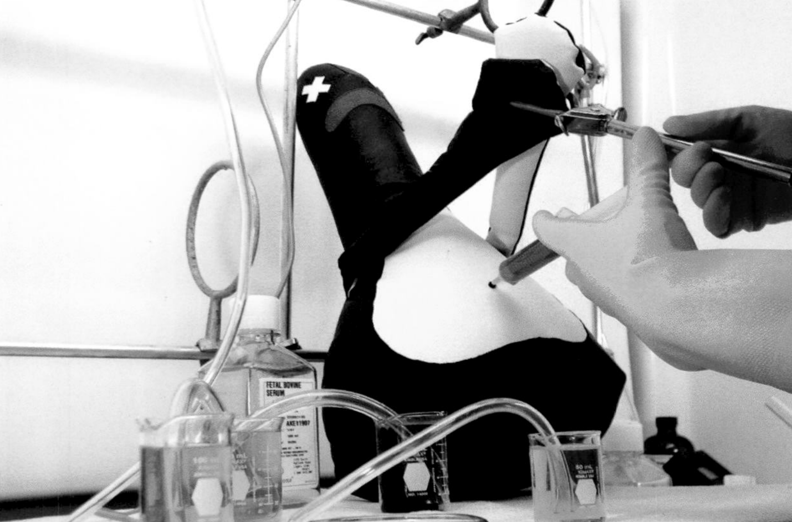
FETAL BOVINE
SERUM

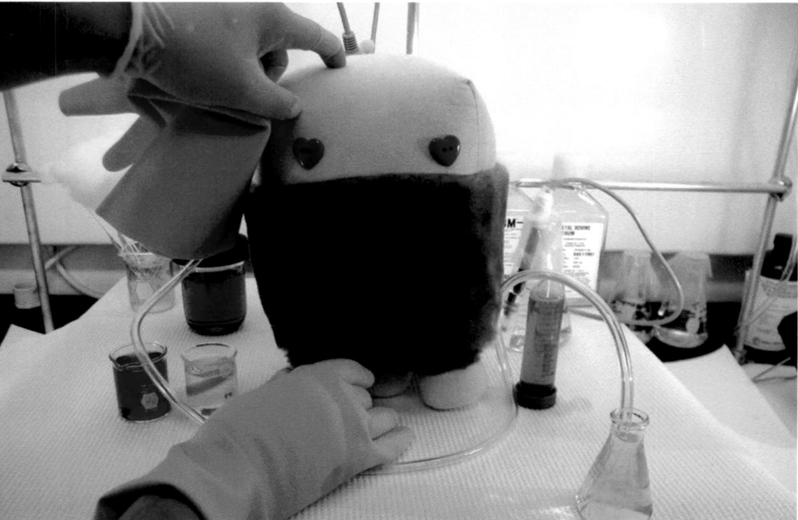

1000 mL

1500 mL
PYREX®
200
400
No. 1000
800

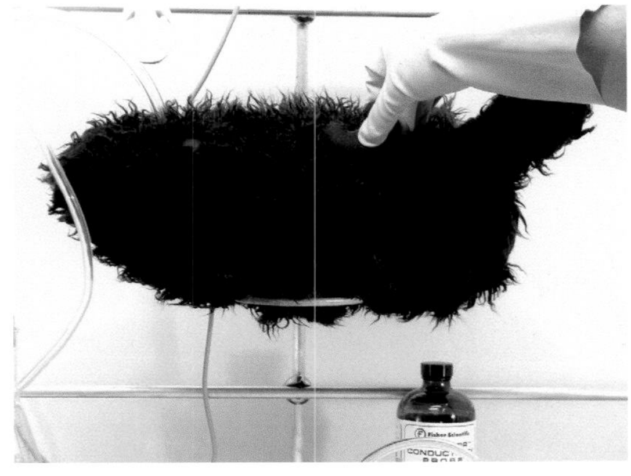

1000 mL
KIMAX
KIMBLE USA
STOPPER NO. 9
EBM-2

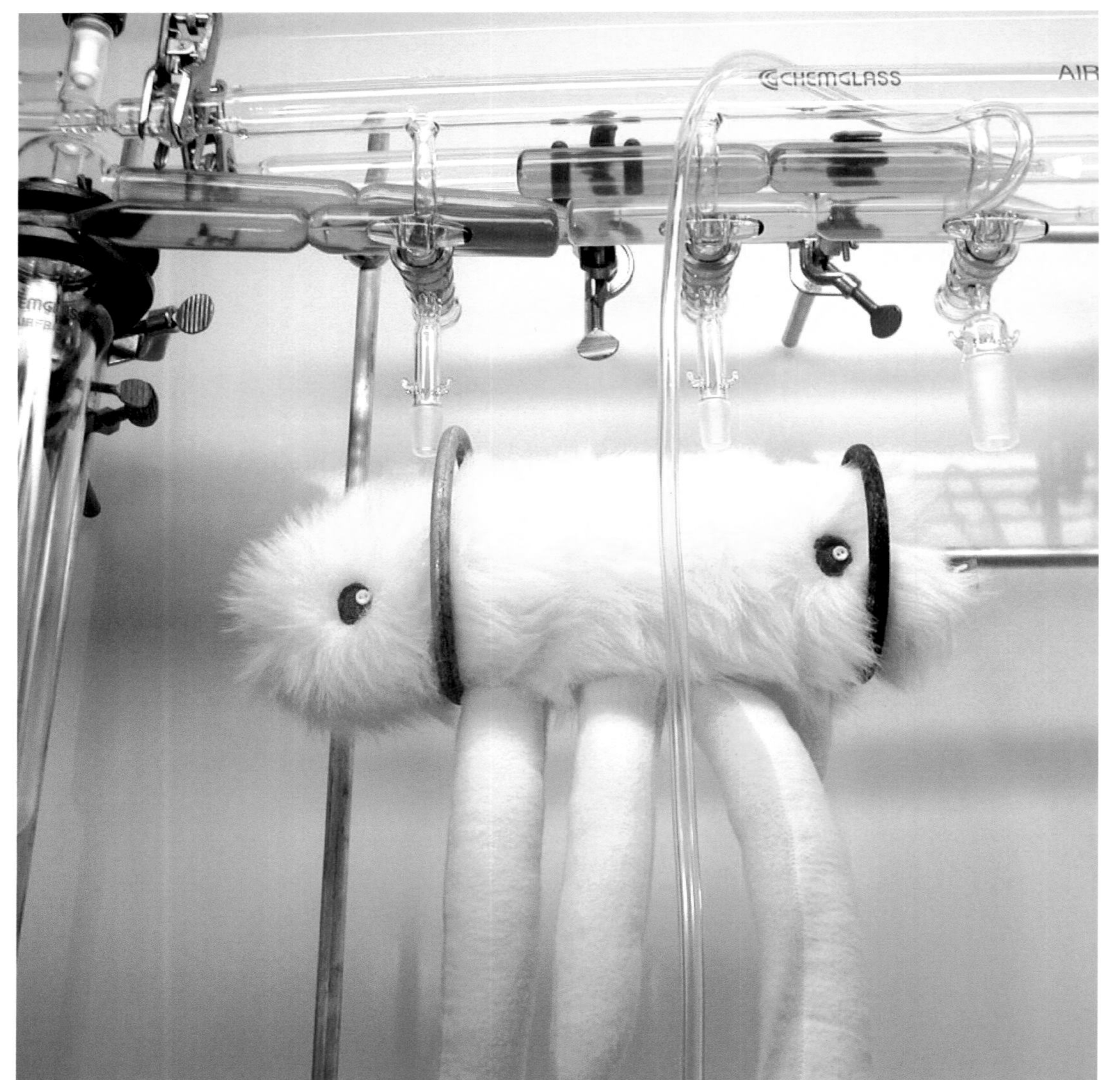
CHEMGLASS
AIR

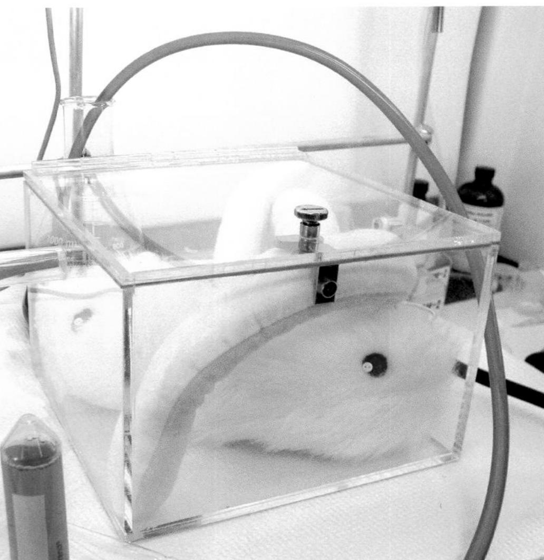

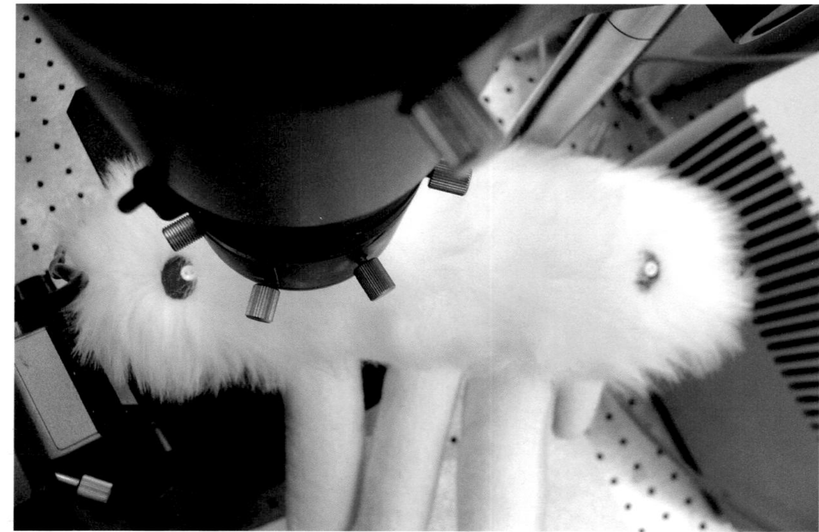

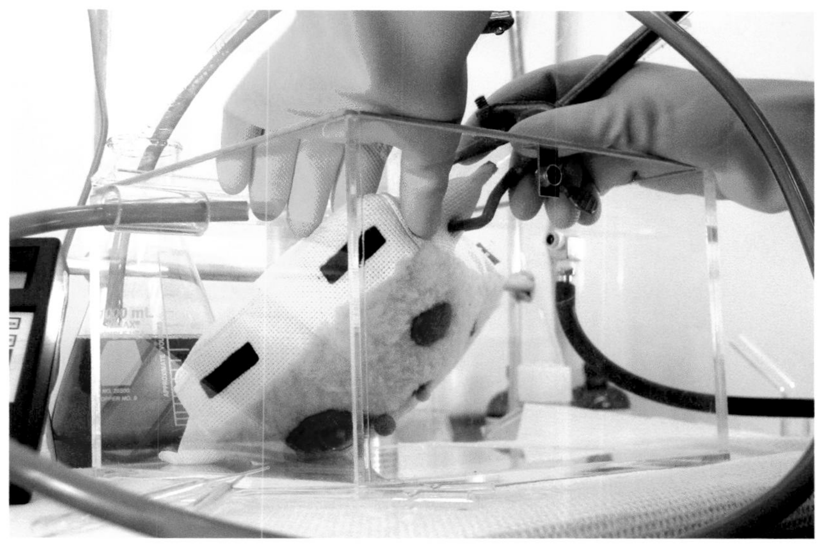

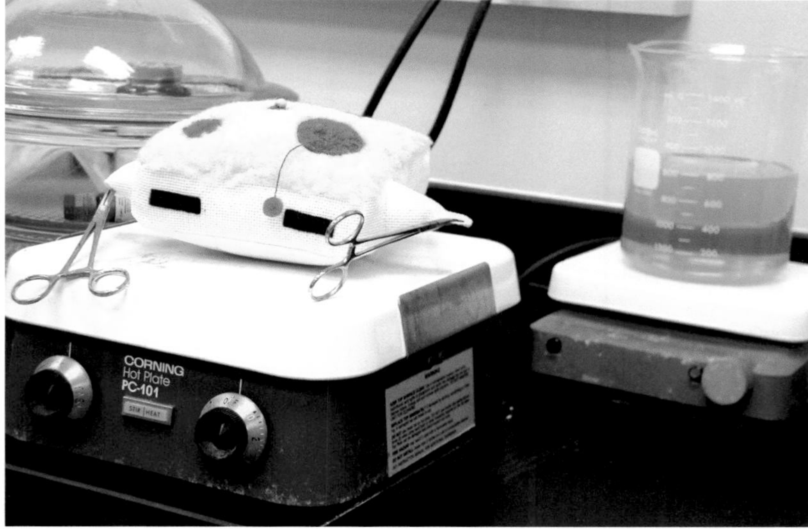
CORNING
Hot Plate
PC-101

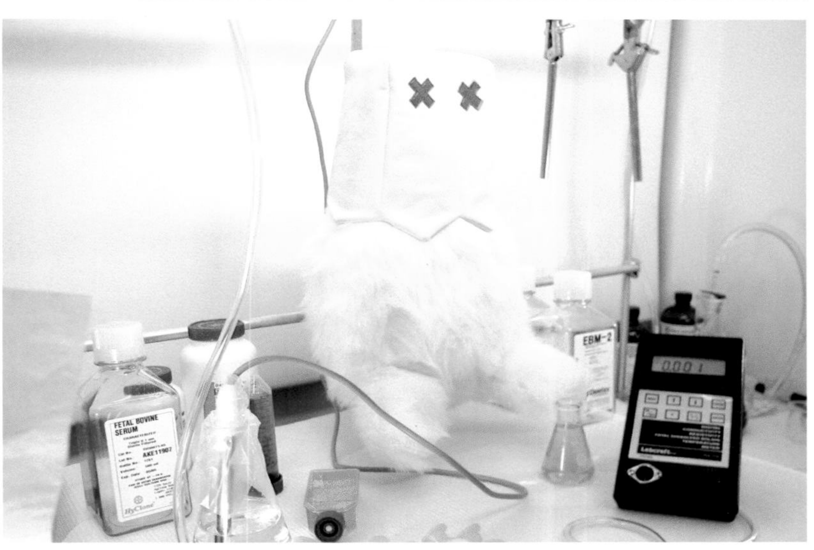
FETAL BOVINE
SERUM
EBM-2
Labcraft

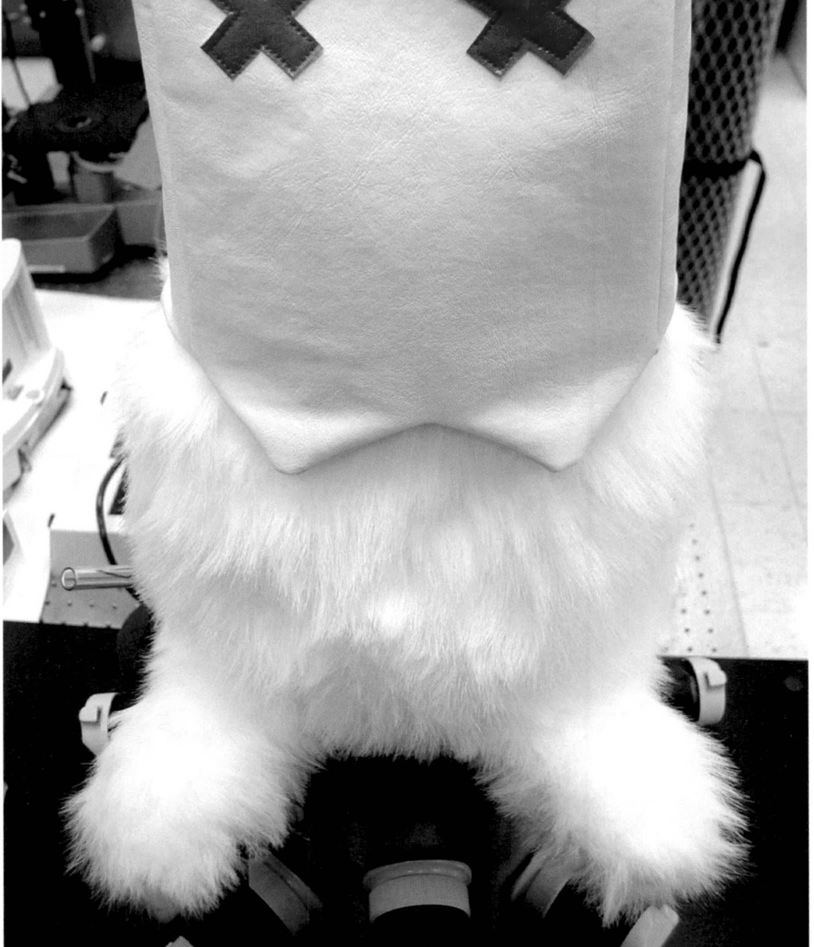

Labcraft

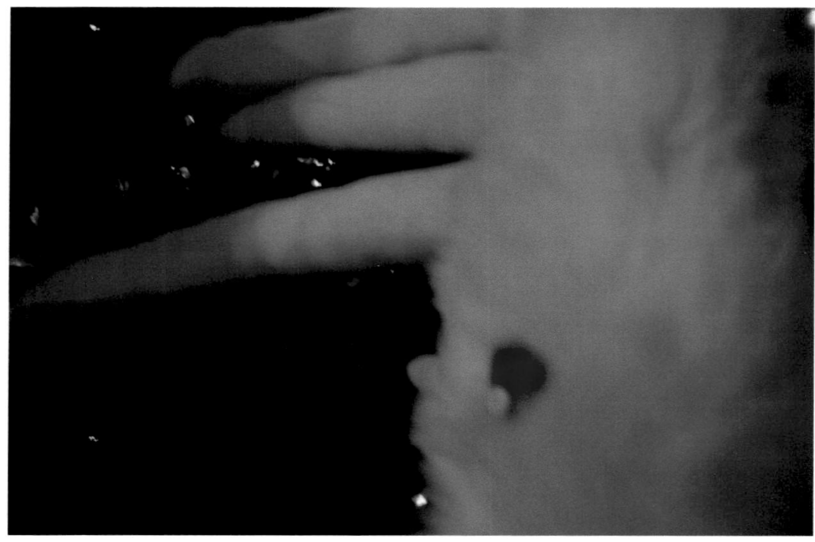

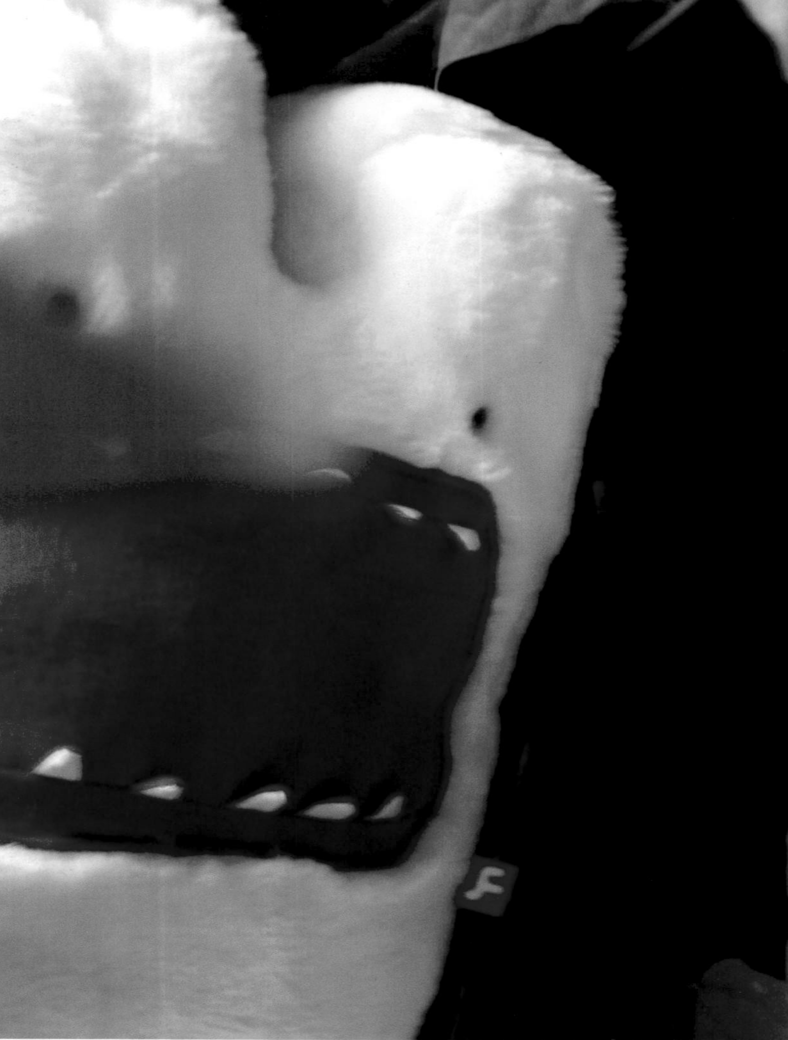

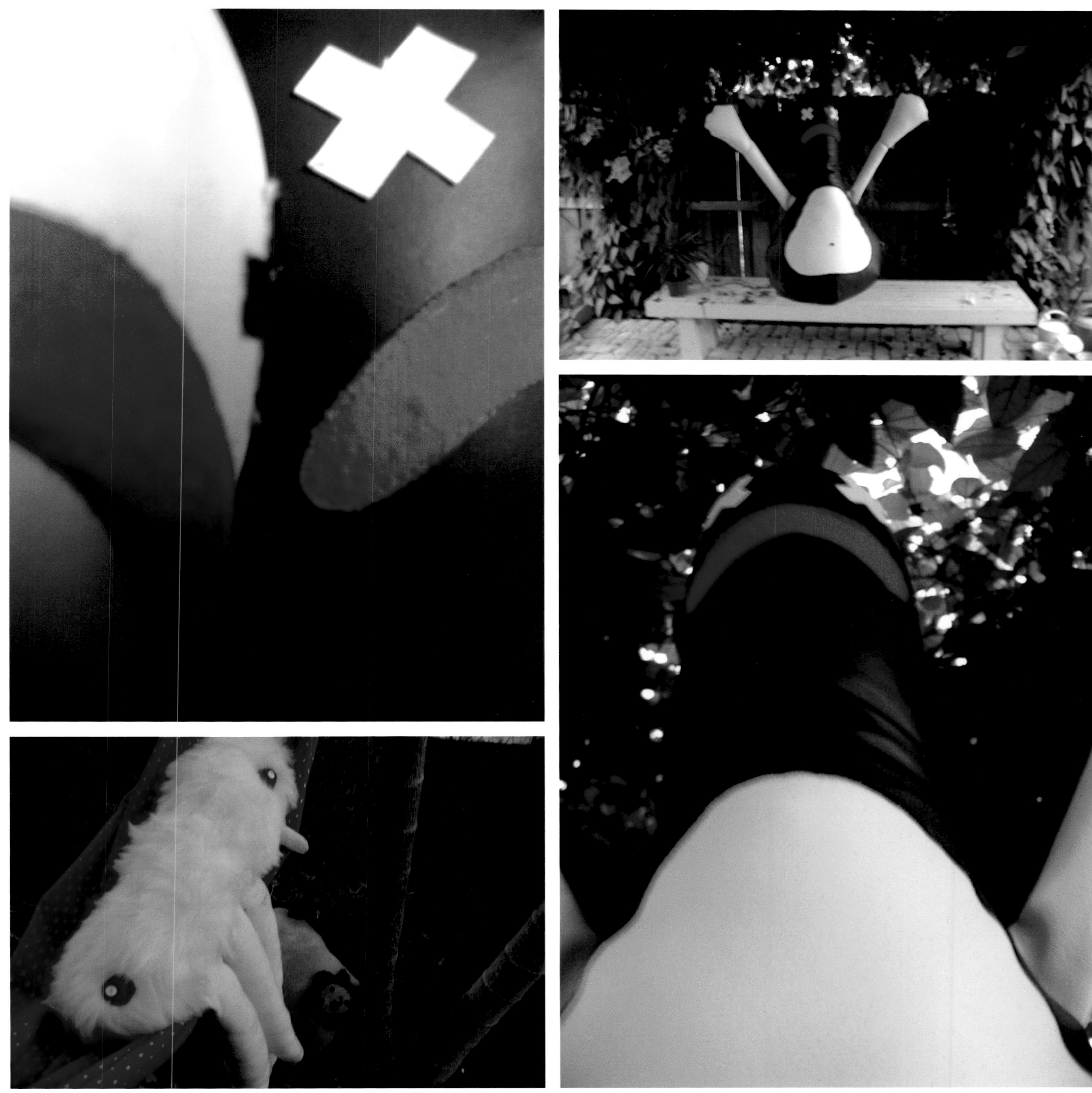

FRIENDS
WITH
YOU
we're here!

FRIENDS
WITH
PRETZ

The Good Wood Gang

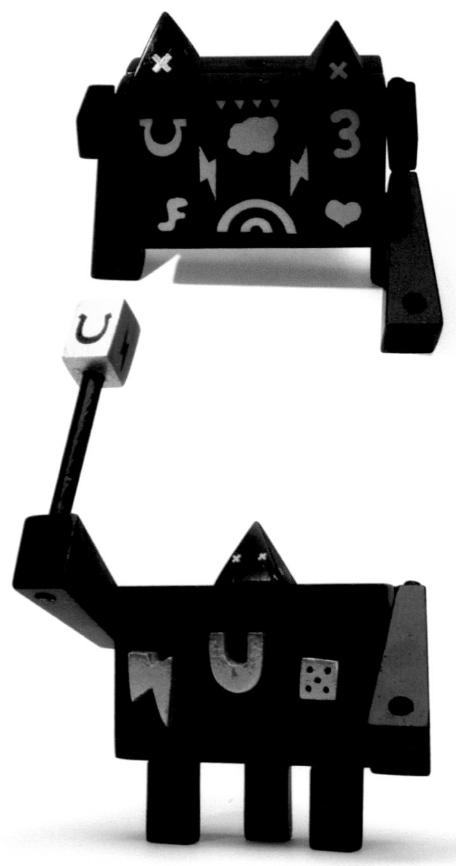

Black Foot (top) – Mr. TTT Burger (bottom)

Lucky Doovoo (top) - Sweet Tooth (bottom)

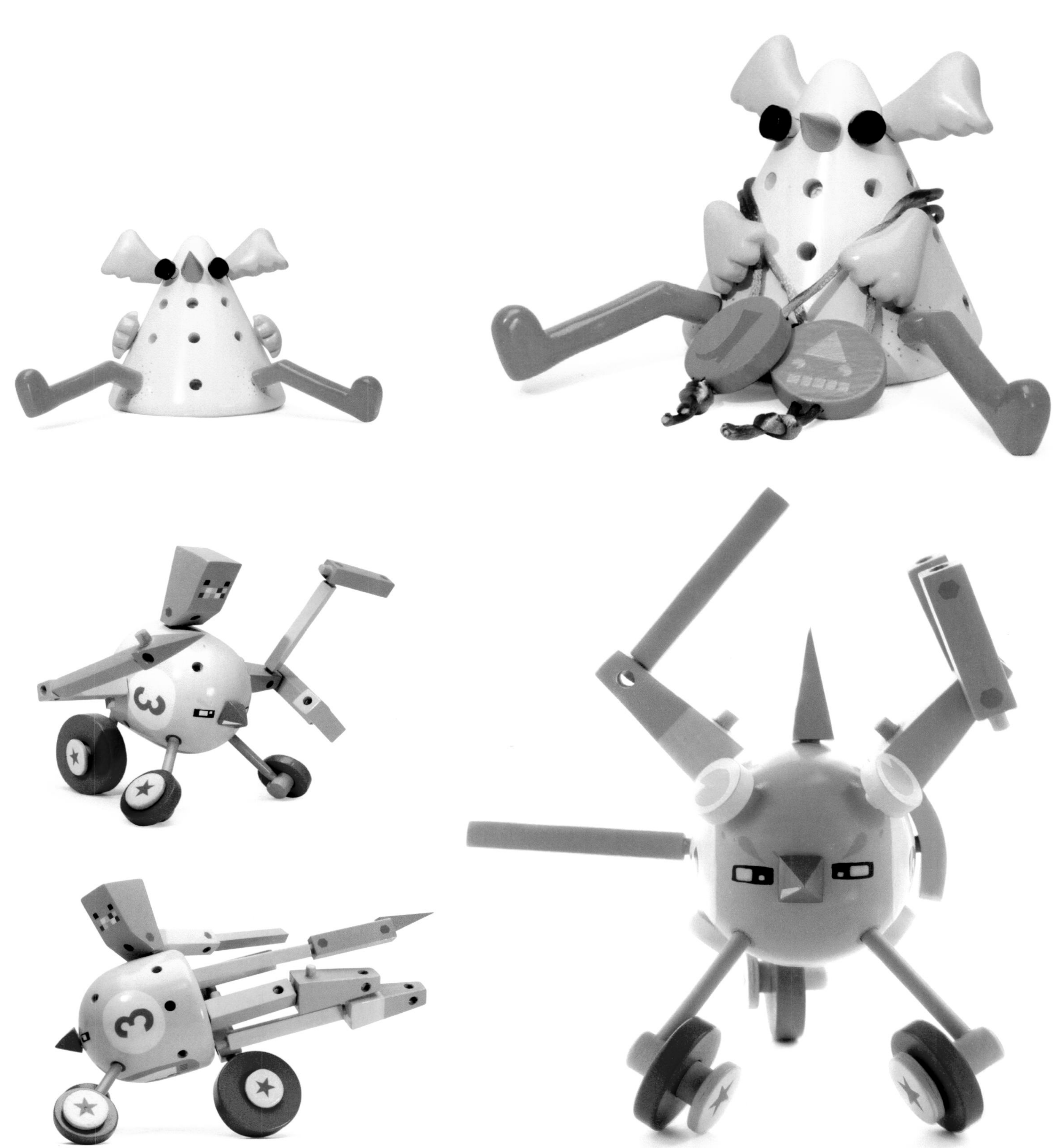

Albirdo (top) - Squid Racer (bottom)

From the Black Forest comes a new type of lucky amulet.
A wooden charm that dates back to the five ancient child gods and the toys that delighted them. They can bring magic and mystery into your life. All have special powers and work in different ways for different people. If you treat them with respect, they will grant you all your wishes. Black Foot aka Captain Bingo opens and closes all doors. Sweet Tooth brings you success and surprises. Lucky Doovoo can solve all your problems, like love, health, distress. Squid Racer, a triple team of power, united to help you achieve your goals and THE rare Mr. TTT BURGER will satisfy all your indulgences and help you to a delicious existence while showing you the key to immortality.

THE
GOOD WOOD
GANG
LUCKY
DOOVOO
0-3
includes one
Power
Ruby
also with one
Magic Heart Amulet
MAGICAL
MODULAR
TOYS
FIVE
CLEVER
WOOD TOYS

THE
GOOD WOOD
GANG
BLACK
FOOT
a.k.a. CAPTIAN BINGO
0-3
Unlock your Luck Today
Divination Amulet
MAGICAL
MODULAR
TOYS
FIVE
CLEVER
WOOD TOYS

THE
GOOD WOOD
GANG
SWEET
TOOTH
BABY DERWIN
Lil' Bernie
MAGICAL
MODULAR
TOYS
FIVE
CLEVER
WOOD TOYS

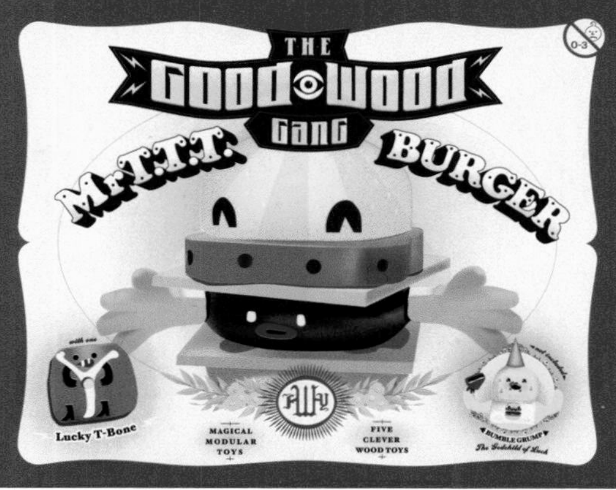
THE
GOOD WOOD
GANG
M.T.T.T.
BURGER
Lucky T-Bone
MAGICAL
MODULAR
TOYS
FIVE
CLEVER
WOOD TOYS

THE
GOOD WOOD
GANG
SQUID
RACER
Singing Robot Head
GOD
OF THE
SEA
MAGICAL
MODULAR
TOYS
FIVE
CLEVER
WOOD TOYS

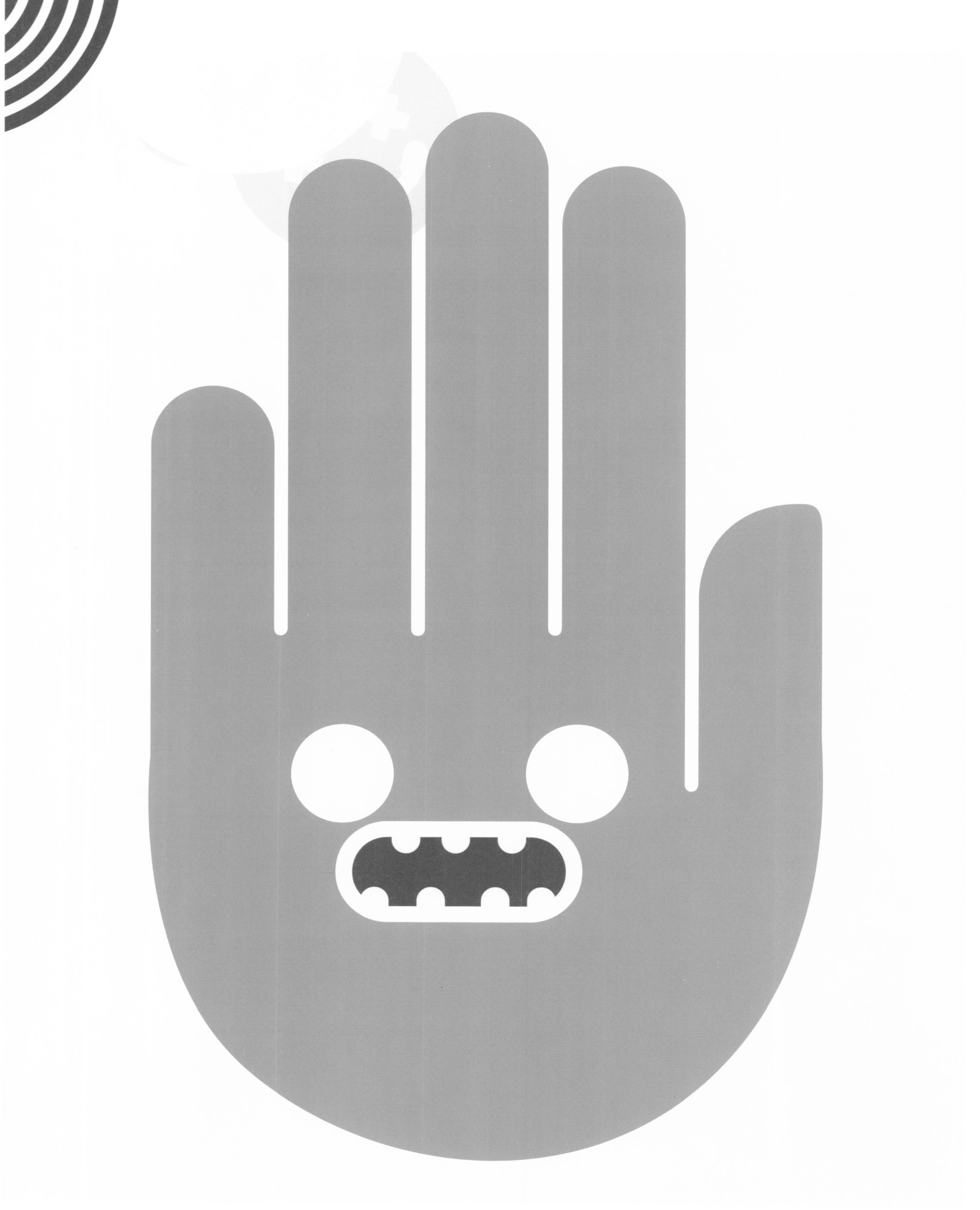

Friends
WITH YOU

the Good Wood Gang!

AMAZING!

5 ORIGINAL WOOD TOYS

MODULAR AND MAGICAL

Real MIGHTY POWER AMULETS

CREATED BY Friends WITH YOU

THE BURGER BUNCH

© Friends With You

Rainbow Valley
8.5 ft.
Stroller Parking
Please take all valuables possessions with you...
Thank you!

Stroller Parking
Please take all valuables possessions with you...
Thank you!

i love hungry

i love hungry

FRIENDSWITHYOU • MAGIC • LUCK • FRIENDSHIP
FRIENDSWITHYOU • MAGIC • LUCK • FRIENDSHIP
wFy
MALFI
XXXX

friends with you
Friends With You

MAGIC
FRIENDSHIP
FRIENDSHIP
MAGIC
LUCK
Friends
WITH YOU

FRIENDS
WITH
YOU
FRIENDS
WITH
YOU
WWW.FRIENDSWITHYOU.COM
Friends
With
You
Malfi
M
FRIENDS WITH YOU
magic
Friends with you
friends
with
you
Friends with You
Friends withyou
FRIENDS WITH YOU
Friends
Friends
with
you
FriendsWithYou
friendly magic
FriendsWithYou...

I ♥ MALFI
MALFI IS YOUR FRIEND!
I ♥ MALFI

FRIENDS with YOU

Friends With You

FRIENDS
WITH
YOU

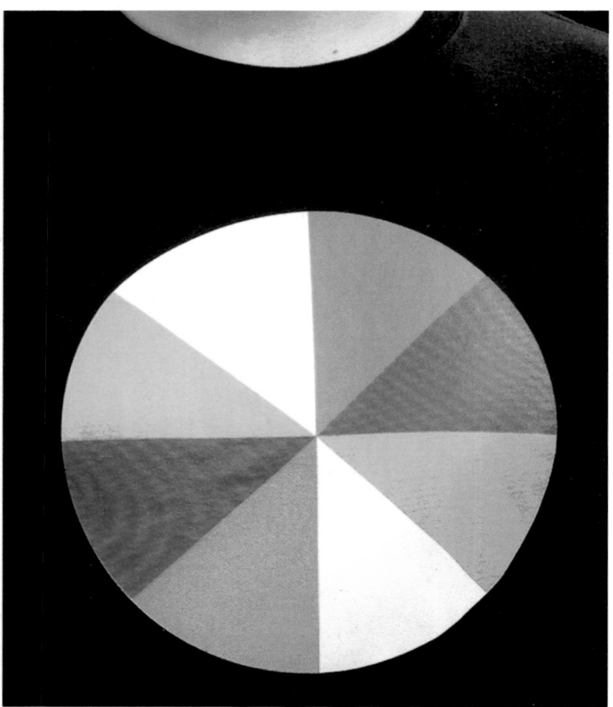

Friends
WITH YOU

FRIENDS
with
YOU

Friends

Real POWER
AMULETS
Friends
WITH YOU

FriendsWithYou

MAGIC

LUCK

FRIENDSHIP

ENJOY
YOUR
LUCK
TUDAY

Friends!
With You

Bite Me

BE HAPPY!

MAGICAL
FRUIT

Friends
with you

MALFI IS
YOUR
FRIEND!

Friends
with you

Friends With You

FRIENDS
WITH YOU

Friends
With You

FriendsWithYou

FRIENDS
WITH YOU

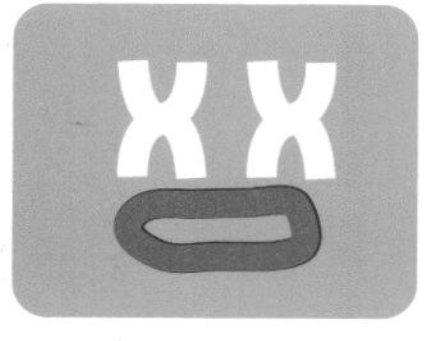

FRIENDS
WITH
YOU

F
by:
Friends With You

BE HAPPY!

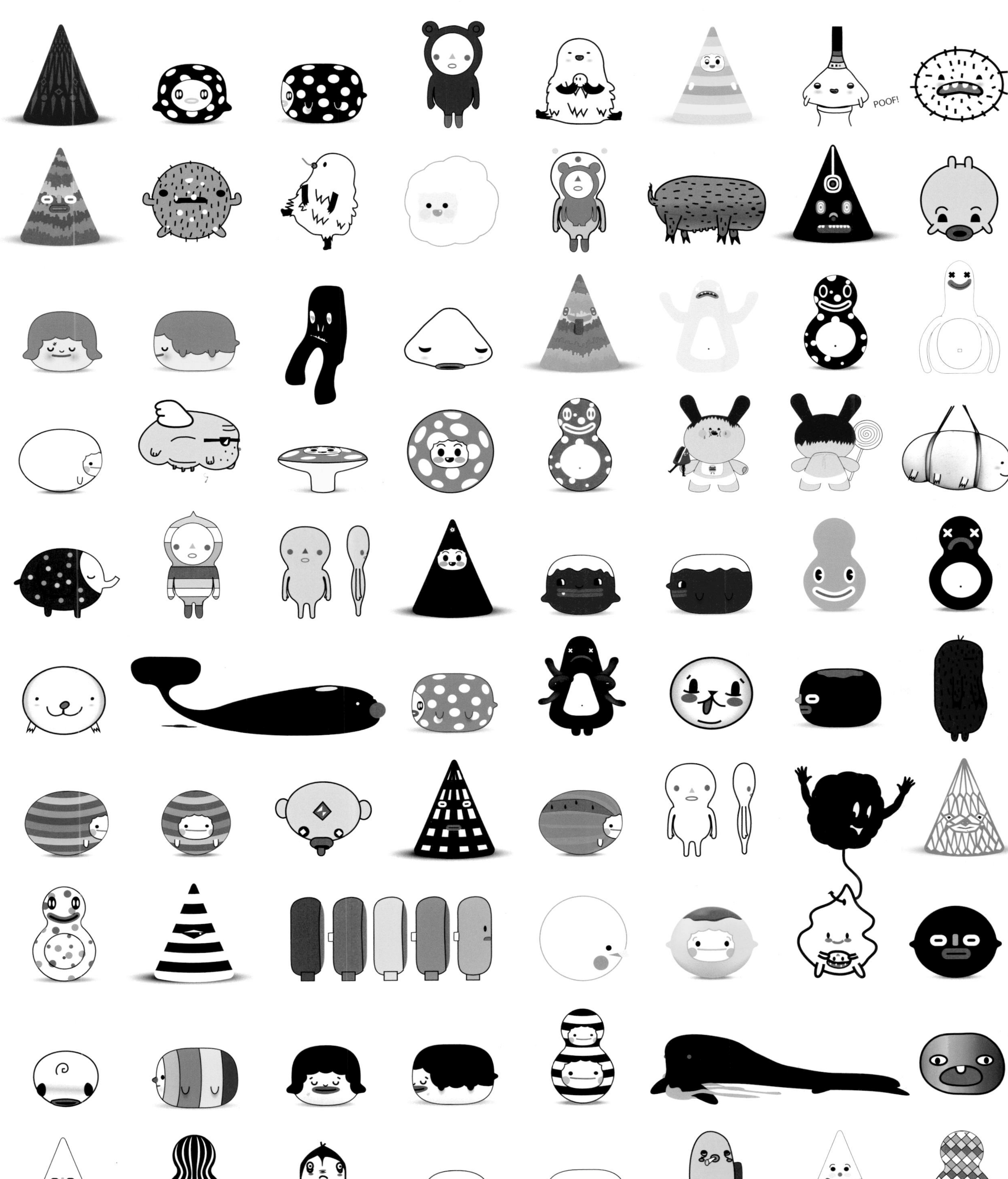
POOF!

FRIEN
WITH

FRiENDS
CHILL
FOTO FOTO FOTO FOTO FOTO FOTO FOTO FOTO FOTO
FRiENDS
13

electric
SHOW
EN
VIVO
JUE
VIE
SAB
DOM
City of Miami Police Department
$10,000
REWARD
CALL 305-579-6630 or
305-471-TIPS (8477)
MAGIC
POP
606

friends with you
FWy
low magic
died

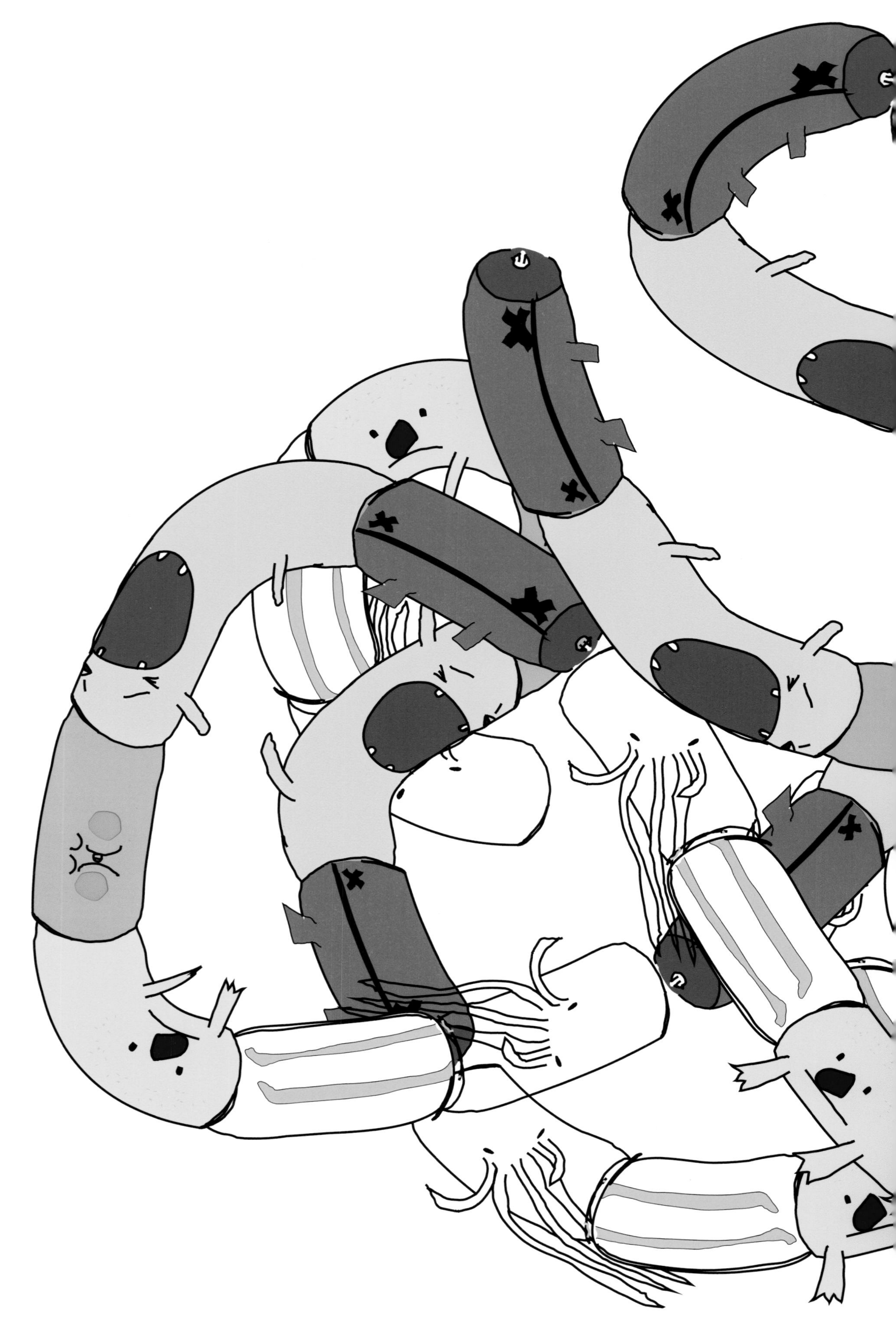

QUI
UMAKI

Remixed by: Phoenecia & Secret Frequency Crew
JANDEK
Your Other Men
schematic
A) Your Other Man (Secret Frequency Crew Remix)
Written by Jandek Remix & Additional Production by Adrian Michna / Raphi Gottesman / Matthew Brown. Recorded at Studio E7, New York City
B) Your Other Man (Phoenecia Outer Harmony)
Written by Jandek Remix & Additional Production by Joshua Kay & Romulo Del Castillo. Recorded at The Humidor, Miami
Schematic Private Press catalog # SCH064 P&C 2005 Schematic Music. ASCAP
Designed by: FriendsWithYou Illustration by: Arturo Sandoval III
Original version of 'Your Other Man' appears on Jandek 'Blue Corpse'.
LP. Corwood Industries catalog # 0753
Limited Edition ____/300

FRIENDS-WITH-YOU

Friends with you

FRIENDS WITH YOU

magic

MAGIC · LUCK · FRIENDSHIP

FRIENDSWITHYOU.COM

MAGIC · LUCK · FRIENDS

FRIENDSWITHYOU

Malfi

M

FRIENDS WITH YOU

FRIENDS WITH YOU

magic

WISH
COME
TRUE

Power Pond is an interactive wishing well installation created for the tenth anniversary celebration of the Museum of Contemporary Art in Miami. It originates from a story about a mythical black snake that traveled through portals. Upon seeing the sacred jewels in the Power Pond, the snake is frozen by their beauty and remains forever to grant wishes. Toss your coins onto the sacred jewels and wish hard. If the wish is just, it will be granted. If the wish is selfish, the wish will be eaten by the black snake. Good luck and be careful.

Power Pond Miami 2006

Project Fox Hotel Fox | Room 102 "King Albino Room" & Room 122 "Heavenly Palace" - Copenhagen 2005

(mixed photos of both rooms)

Welcome to the magical world of FriendsWithYou. We are delighted to have you as our guest and will make your stay an adventure. Rest comfortably inside the lurking jaws of, his majesty, King Albino and realize that you are safe as a fluffy cloud. Here is a place to harness good energy, regain your youthfulness and rest blissfully.

You have entered heaven. The Heavenly Palace, although seemingly small is our version of the entire universe. In fact, you are accompanied by a representation of the universe itself, Red Flyer. This room has all the charms and utilities you´d expect from a modernized heaven. So please enjoy being at one with the universe at least for a couple of days.

Project Fox Hotel Fox | Room 214 "Two Swans (Fertility Shrine)" - Copenhagen 2005

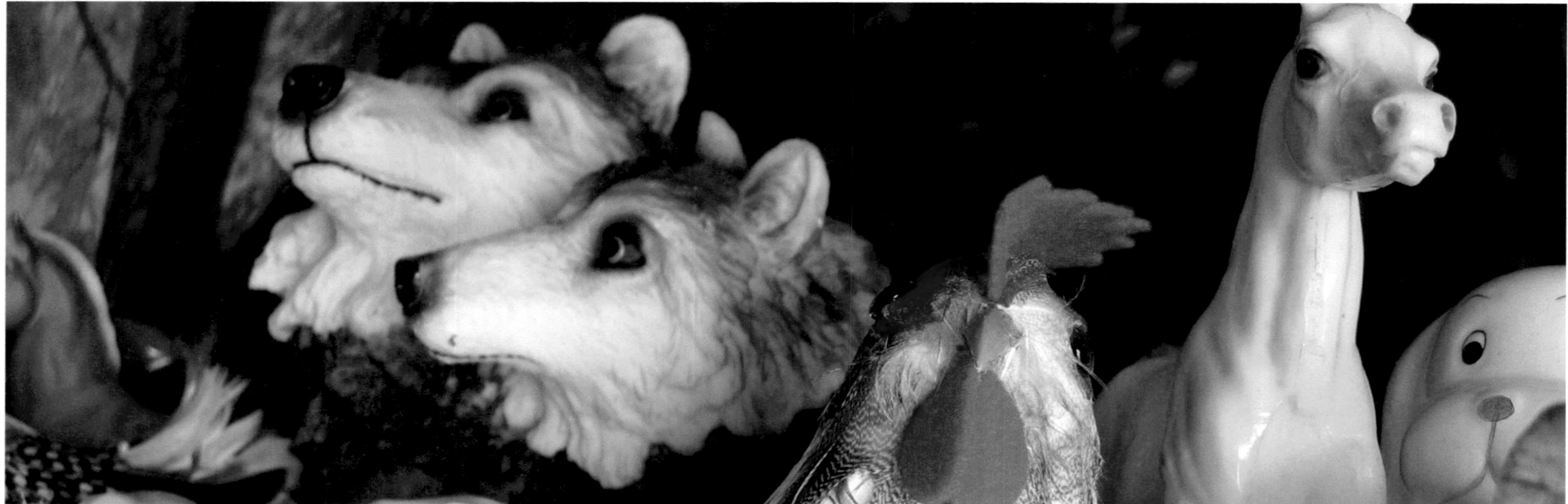

Welcome to your carnal self. We take this opportunity to reacquaint you with your natural creative instincts. Celebrate life, and free yourself from your daily inhibitions. Let the gentle ambience of this sacred forest be your guide, as you slip into your true selves. You may never want to leave.

SAMSUNG

Welcome to the center of the universe! We offer you solace and purity as you enter Harmony's Helm. This room's ultimate soul is revealed once the sacred "Harmony Bell" is used, that is, if you can find it. This is a place where secrets can be revealed internally and literally. Exploration will award you with an assessment of your personal state of being; your goal is to regain honesty through concentration. What are you searching for?

Project Fox The Albino Car (exterior) - Copenhagen 2005

FriendsWithYou was given the task of giving a life, and virtually a soul to the first car ever. Through a special ritual and offerings, we turned soemthing that was metal and gears, into a living creature, and we appeased him with his favorite delights, cakes, flowers and everyhting nice. The Albino Car's inside, is a beautiful bouquet of flowers, fruits and fish, with shiny pink interior, spirits and working lights to keep his heart and belly full of love.

Project Fox The Albino Car (inside) - Copenhagen, 2005

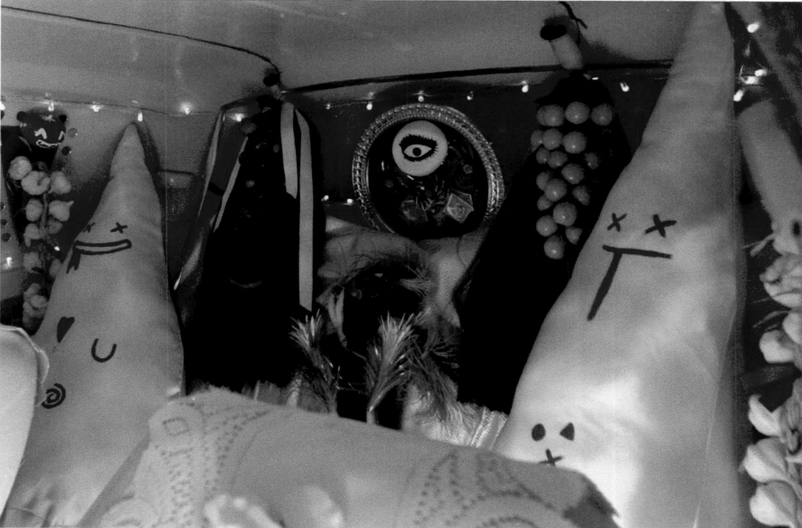

Treasure Whale

The Wizard carried the Whale for many years until he burst, and from him came new baby whales to spread the magic to the entire world, with diamonds and a single golden horseshoe.

Russian Doll Show Portland 2003

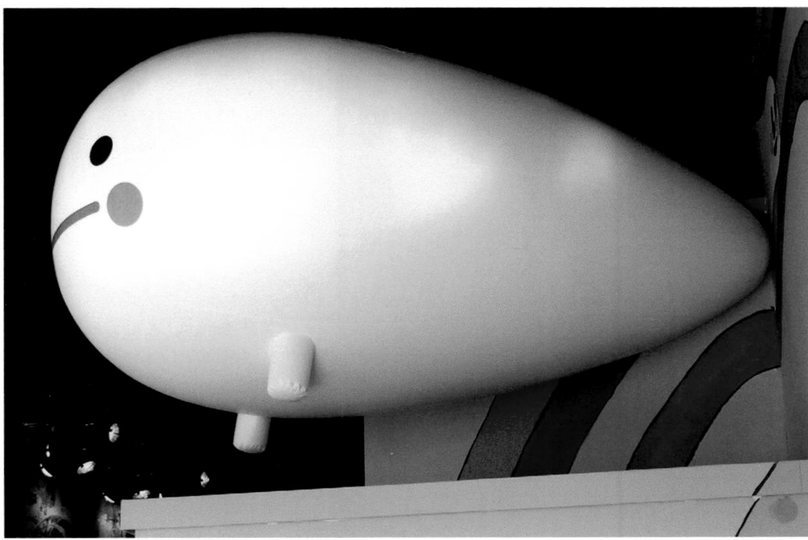

Cloud City Miami 2005

Cloud City is a surreal playground we created where you can act freely and lose sight of your age, ultimately regaining the spirit of your youth where play is inevitable and unrestricted. The main character you meet is a lost spirit called "the boy", who represents the childlike feeling you get when losing sight of society's norms in respect to behavior and play. He will run with you, slide with you. You can push him and shove him. You can even take him home! Buy the boy and play forever! Join the boy and his friends in a magical romp around our world and regain his spirit in your life.

by: FriendsWithYou
FiND!
THE FUN PALACE!
GO NOW!
404 NW 26 St.
HEY!
OPEN DEC 1
A-BRAND-NEW
- Play Ground -
FOR • ALL • TO • PLAY
CLOUD
CITY

Hanging By a Thread Miami 2005

The Boo Boo Boys are sleeping boy spirits. They represent the entire range of human emotion, from the deepest of hatred to the calmest warm feeling. Once they are awakened by the sacred bells, they will decipher your wish and weigh its value to you and the universe. Then, the Boo Boo Boys will either grant your wish or take one of your dreams away. It's your decision! Weigh your thoughts and desires carefully. Good Luck!

I could be nice and not yell

I wish that I will become a famous fashion designer

Living Alive

I wish that Hillary Clinton is our next prez.

Conversation is love.

I wish i get a 2nd better job...

I wish SAM TURNER INTO BISCUIT AND FOR WORLD PIECE! NOT MY LIMBS

I wish to be friends w/ you!!

I WISH FOR MORE CUTE BOYS

To have fun all the time

FREEDOM

A new job OR Rich husband

I wish that I would never get another hemoroid

I WISH TO BE HAPPY & DEBT FREE

I wish Bush didn't hate black people

to love!

give me a path to follow! I need help

I wish to be successful and innovative in the interior design industry. I wish to lead the way in Green buildings. I wish my sister has the most beautiful child.

I WISH FOR JUSTICE

$ $MONEY$ $

VERY little NO CONFLICT with PARTNER IN LIFE.

Fuzzy Puzzy

BE ME AGAIN! BEING WISE ON SETTING MY GOALS

EGG SHELLS AND BROKEN CURTAINS.

I wish for my Mr. Right!

I wish that my mom finds true love w/ a man. He will treat her like a queen. Shenica Randolph

INSPIRATION

THAT'S WHAT I WISH

Effectiveness

Good fortune

To play with my friends

Please kill me

I wish to be happy, healthy, + beautiful inside and out.

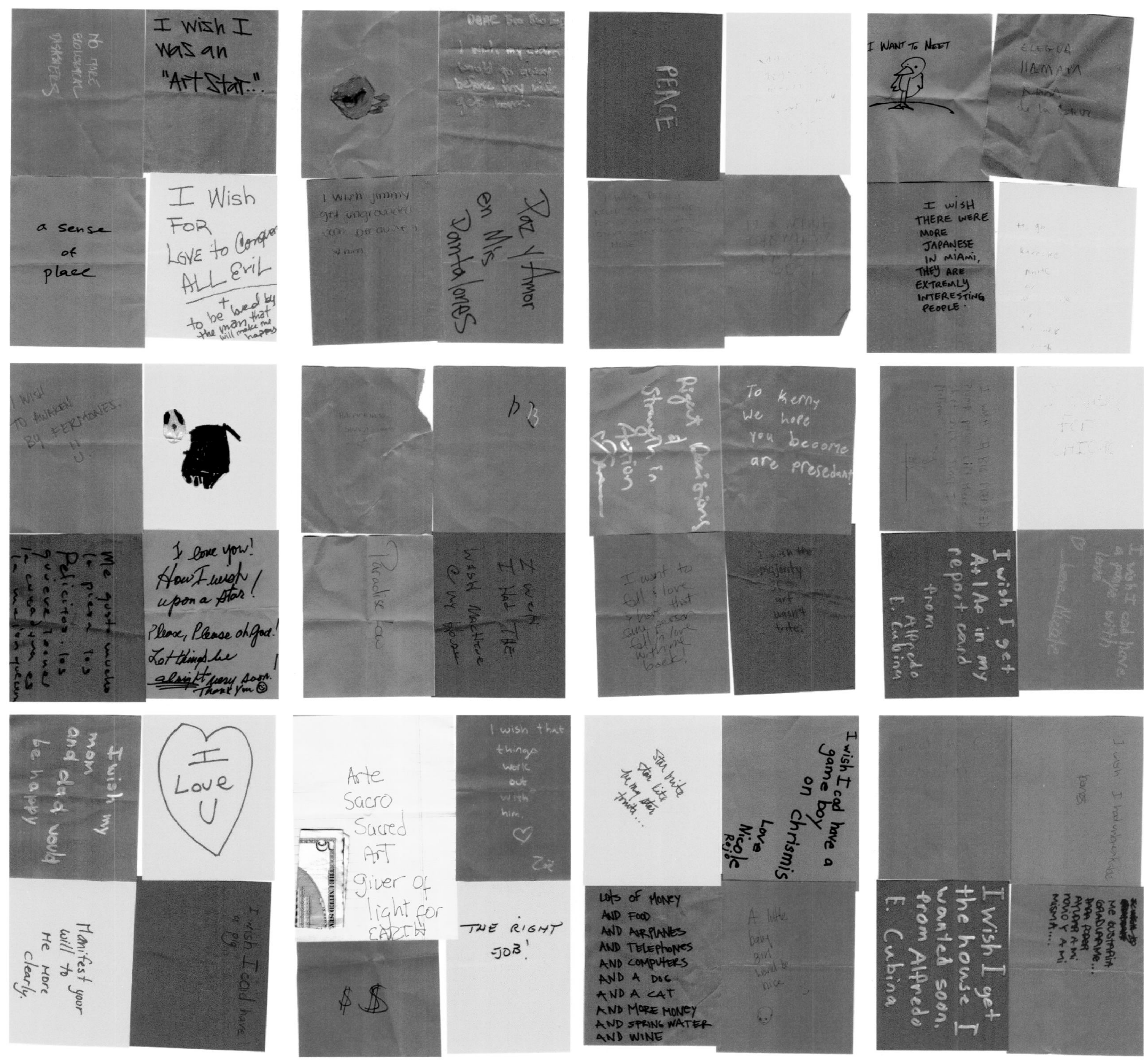

I wish I was an "Art Star"...
PEACE
I WANT TO MEET
a sense of place
I Wish FOR LOVE to
ALL Evil
+ to be loved by the man that will make me happy
Paz y Amor
I WISH THERE WERE MORE JAPANESE IN MIAMI, THEY ARE EXTREMLY INTERESTING PEOPLE.
To Kerny we hope you become are presedent
I love you! How I wish upon a star! Please, Please oh God! Let things be alright very soon. Thank You
I want to fall i love
I wish I get A+1 As in my report card from Alfredo E. Cubina
I wish my mom and dad would be happy
I Love U
Arte Sacro Sacred Art giver of light for EARTH
I wish that things work out with him. Zoë
I wish I cod have a game boy on Chrismis
Love Nicole Rojo
Manifest your will to me more clearly.
I wish I cod have
THE RIGHT JOB!
$ $
LOTS OF MONEY AND FOOD AND AIRPLANES AND TELEPHONES AND COMPUTERS AND A DOG AND A CAT AND MORE MONEY AND SPRING WATER AND WINE
I wish I get the house I wanted soon. from Alfredo E. Cubina

See this and die Miami 2005

This was an installation with hundreds of spirits floating into the sky! If you saw them, you might be entranced to follow!

Get Lucky Miami & Los Angeles 2004

“Get Lucky” is an adventure into a modern ritual that empowers us to realize the significant effect we can pose on the world, and a chance to alter it to a more balanced state to achieve happiness. We will provide a quick wish response system, face-to-face time with God, and multiple sub Gods in order to accommodate the aspects of our lives that we strive to better. No more wasteful prayers, no more disappointments. Get ready to experience a fast connection with the abstract being inside us all, the unification of human, animal and nature. The “Fur Liaison” will act as a tour guide, and help you accept the trials and tribulations of your daily life. Good luck and be careful.

WHITE WIZARD KING represents the white powers of the world, keeping order by maintaining the world's structure in harmony, continually tipping the scales between good and evil. This Wizard is in ultimate opposition of the BLACK SERPENT KING, and works to fix all the actions of him. Super Powers include; Magic beam of Kindness, and double SUPER SPIRIT BLAST.

DOUBLE WEALTH WIZARD Give to Get! Got no money? Well, GIVE IT TO US! Stop gambling or giving it away to investments, this even works better than the lottery! This is your chance to be rich; this is your chance to get ahead. Want POWER, how about some HOT SEX! You can buy anything you want with the help of SUPER WEALTH WIZARD.

BLACK SERPENT KING, "RULER OF CHAOS" represents the dark end of the world. He is the passion, for excellence and undying hunger, pain and suffering, reward and desire. He is a lord of mischief and hysteria and good luck. He represents the natural instincts that exist inside us: sex, money, fame, and power. The dark side contains the ultimate of all powers and is in constant opposition of the WHITE WIZARD KING.

GOD of LOVE AND BEAUTY represents the ultimate human condition, representing love and lack thereof. Beyond all other factors this remains what shapes how our lives are shaped. You can either have love in your heart or always be searching for it. This magic podium offers you unconditional love and the ability to accept it.

SUPER SANGRE SHAMAN is the guardian of all life. His pictures represent the immediate people he is thinking of, until they pass on and the pictures change. He works hard and watches mercifully, giving and taking lives. He regulates the intricate system and blood flow inside all creatures. When he usurps your life he will extract your energy by turning it into bubbles and redirect it to its next journey.

TIERRA MADRE - Earth is the creator of man, nature and animal. Inside our planet is a star, burning and heating the world day after day. From the ocean came life and from her volcanoes came land. We are all maintained by her whim and often take all her gifts for granted. Pay your respect, and learn how to recycle. Make sure to greet animals and fellow humans as equals. WE ARE ALL CONNECTED!

Aqui Uzumaki Tokyo 2004

A multimedia installation by FriendsWithYou, Mumbleboy and Gaga Inc. at Hanna Gallery in Tokyo, Japan. Roughly translated from a Japanese-Spanish concoction meaning 'Here is Vortex,' the show features a wall to wall plastering of collaborative drawings, a musical soundtrack, visuals and motion graphics created by the artists. The show's centerpiece is an oversized tornado of special edition plush dolls, handmade specifically for the event.

EEP BACK
200 FEET
evor
NYC
大江戸

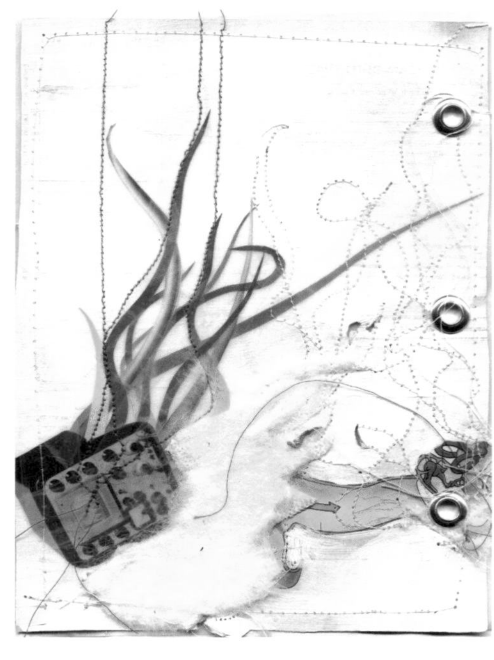

NATUR

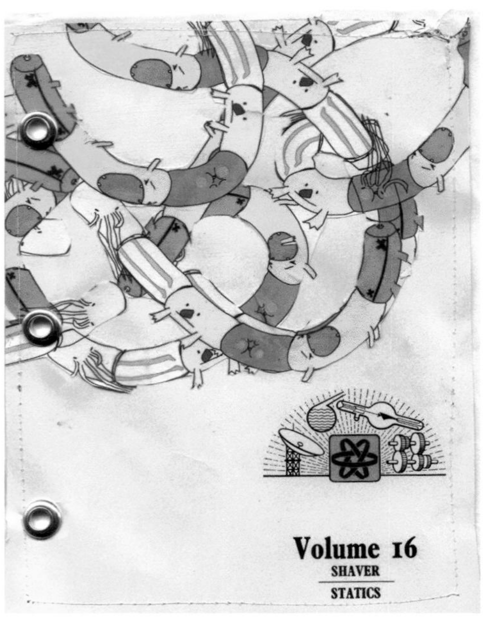
Volume 16
SHAVER
STATICS

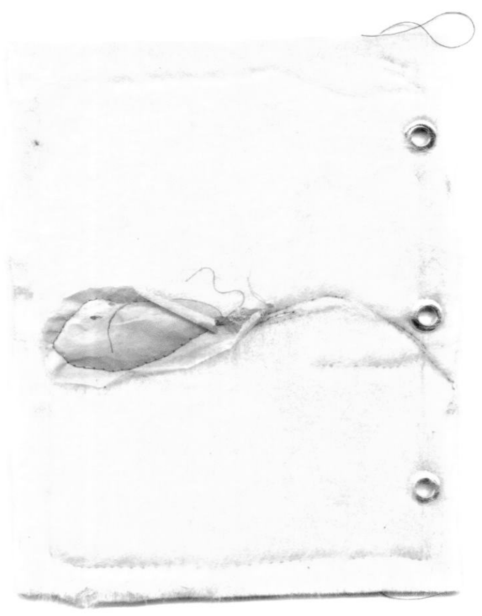

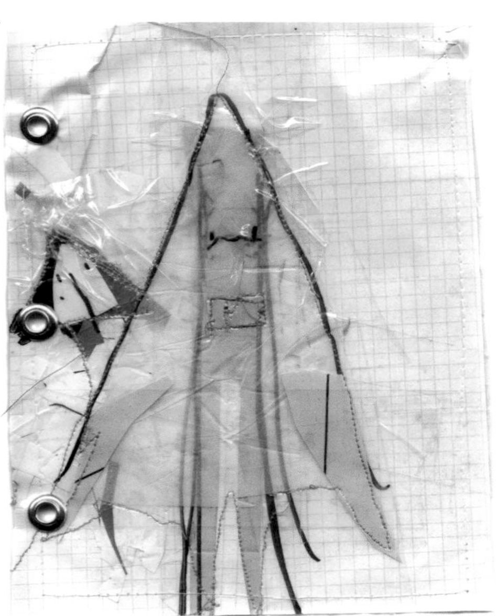

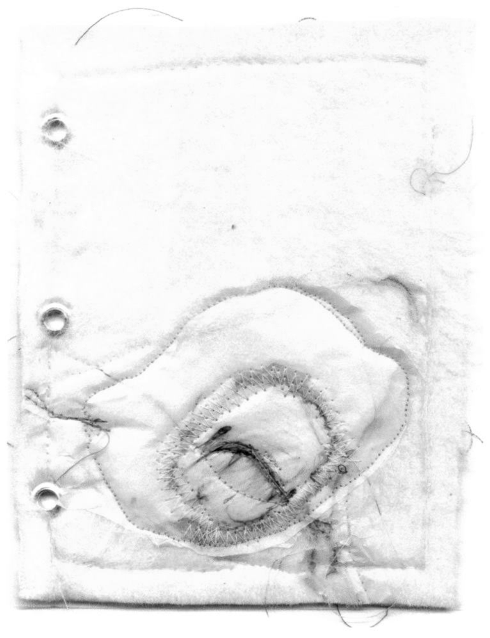

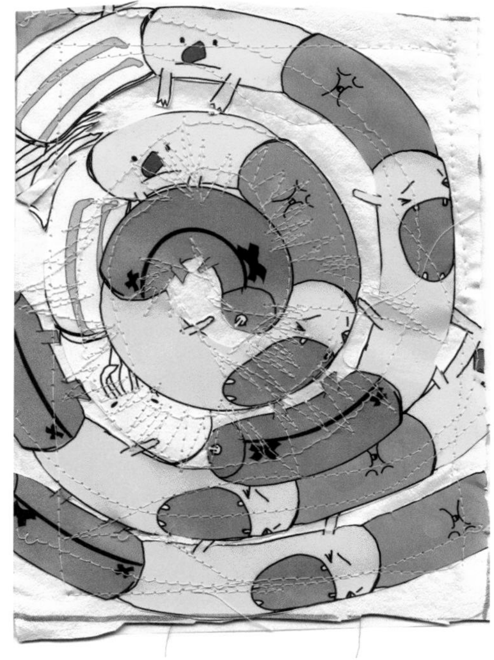

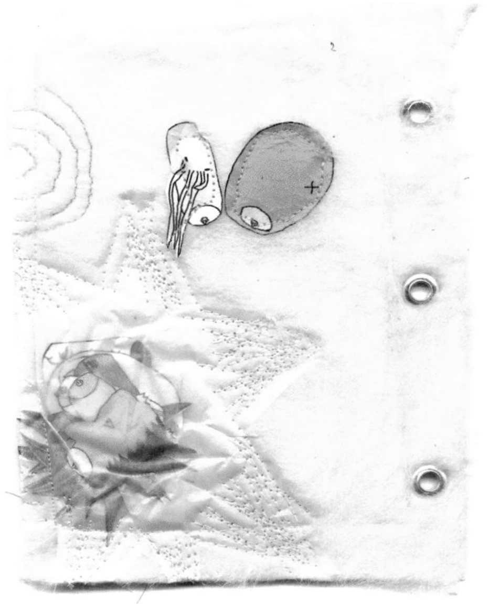

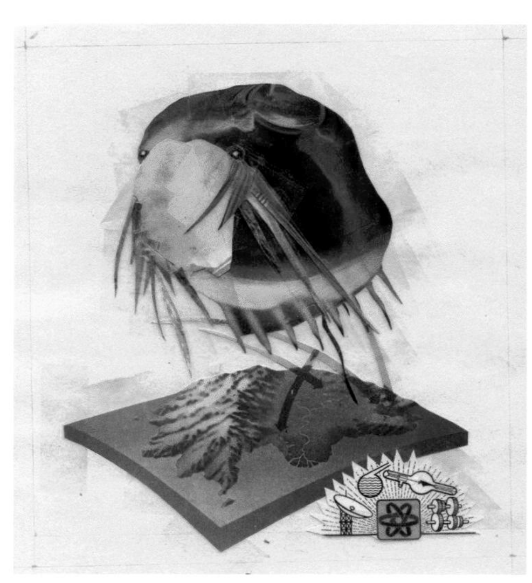

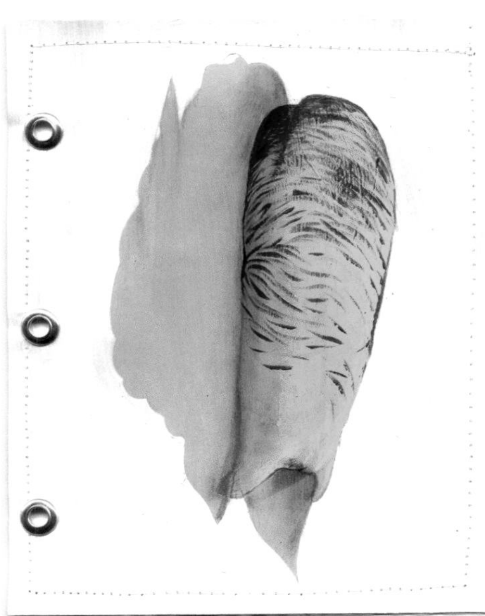

A

E

$
MAGIC

THE CITY OF MIAMI
INCORPORATED
1896
DADE CO., FLORIDA

2417
REESE STUDIO

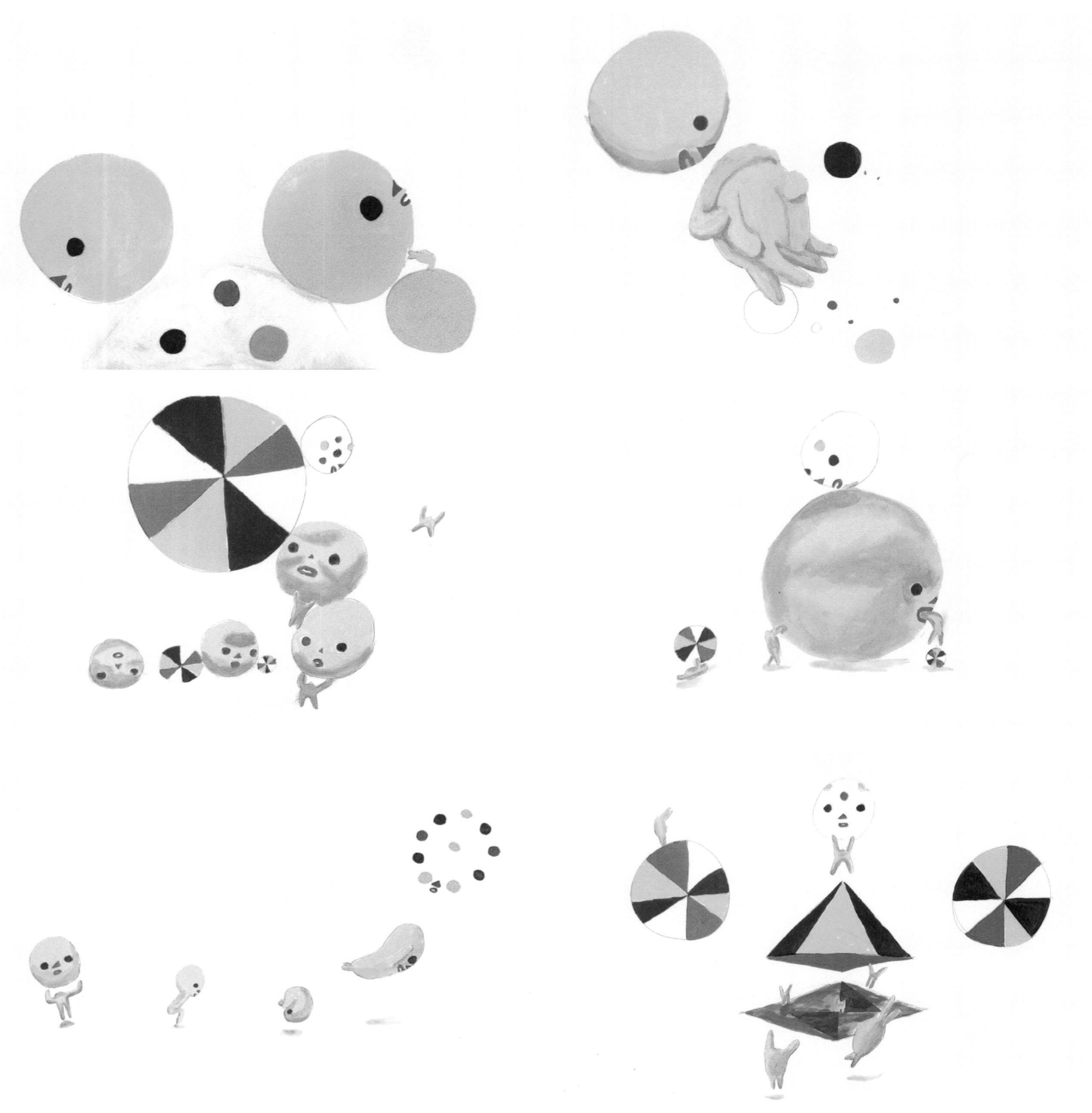

SAM06

PETERS & KEMP.

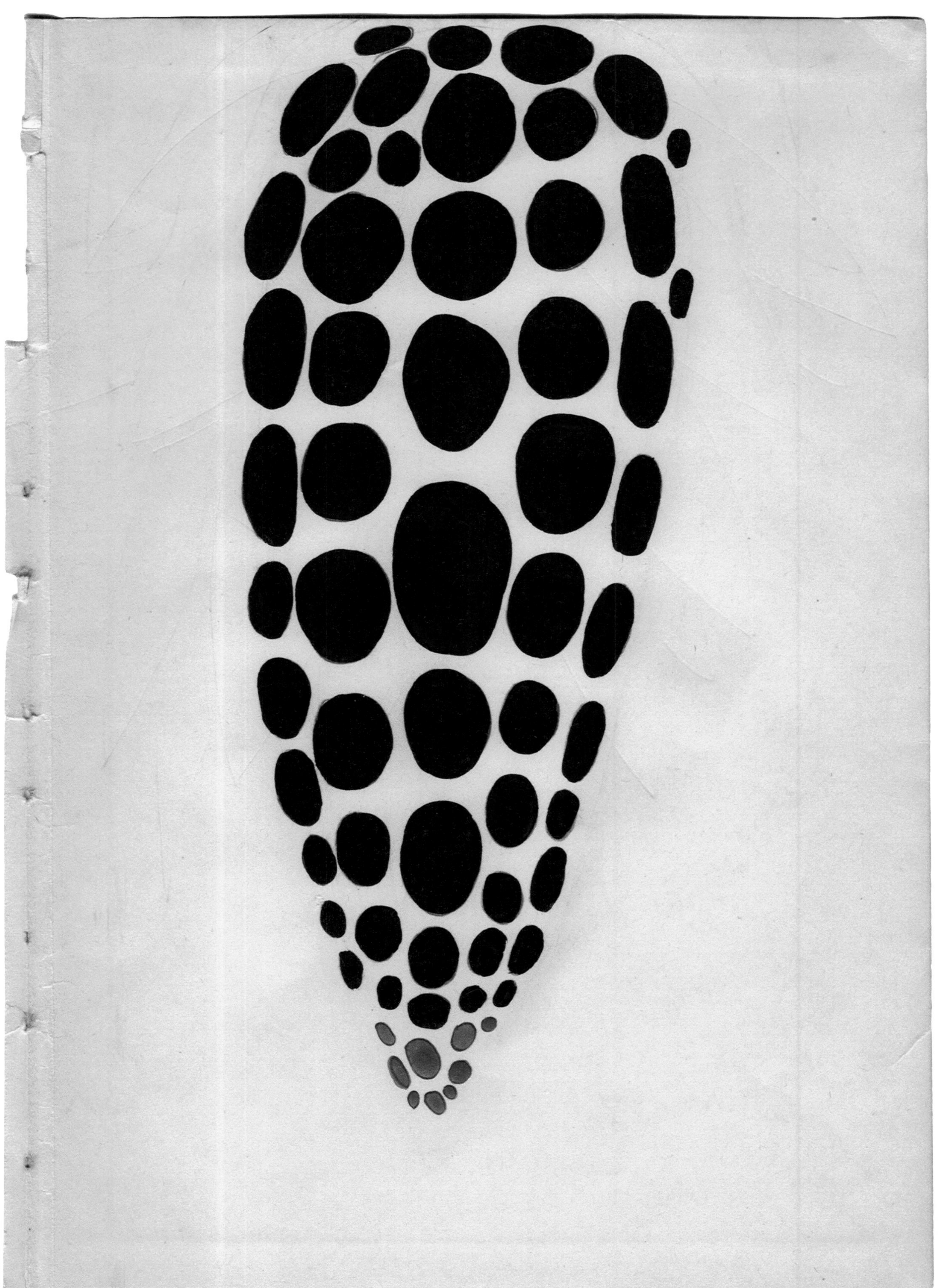

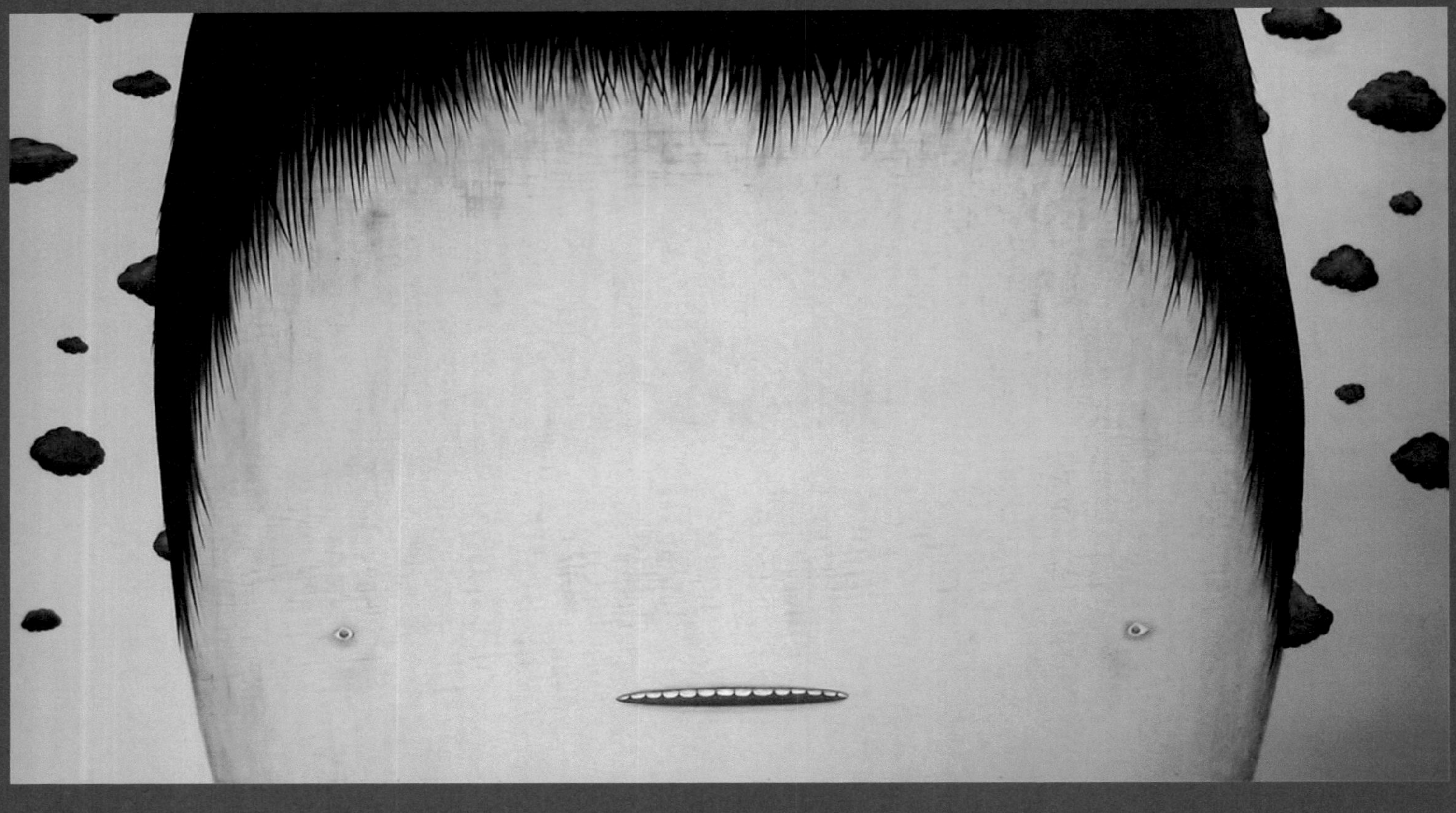

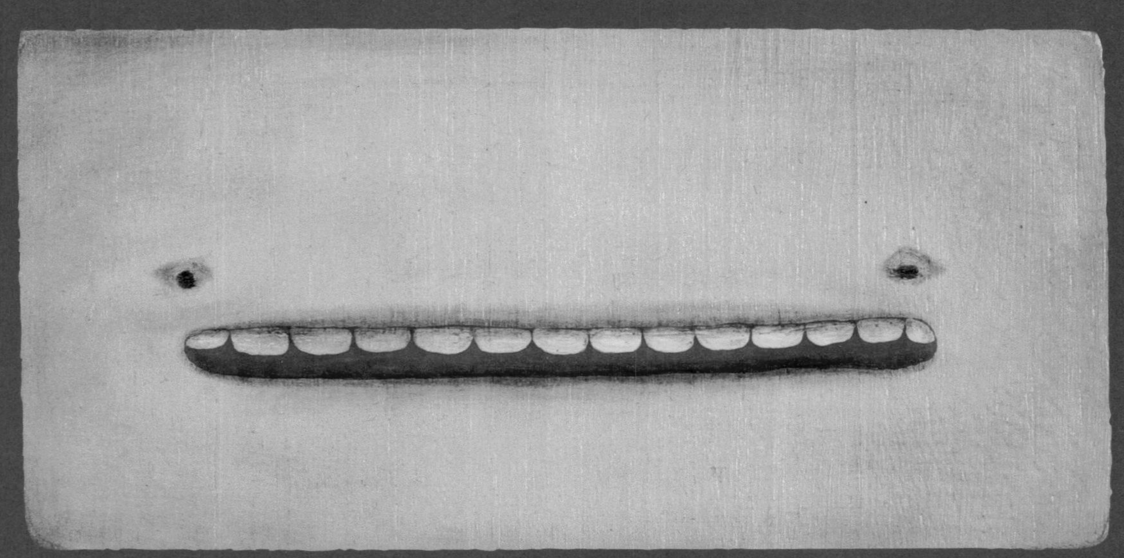

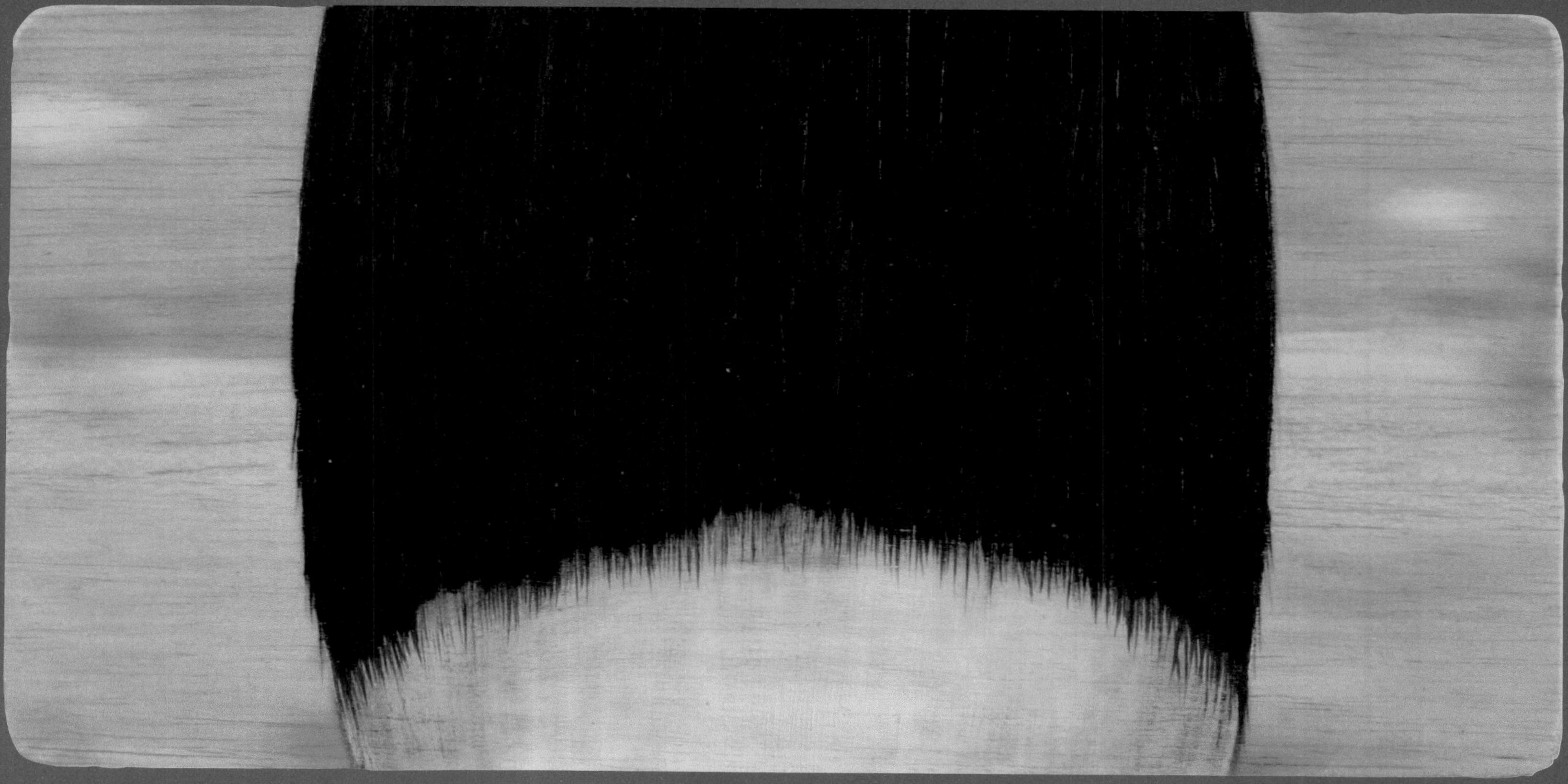

LIFE WORLD LIBRARY
ISRAEL

LIFE NATURE LIBRARY
THE
MOUNTAINS

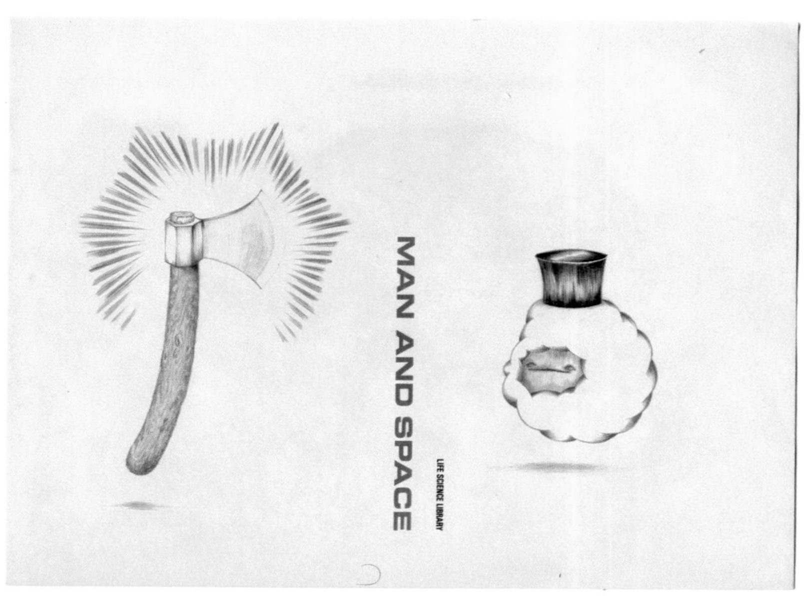
MAN AND SPACE
LIFE SCIENCE LIBRARY

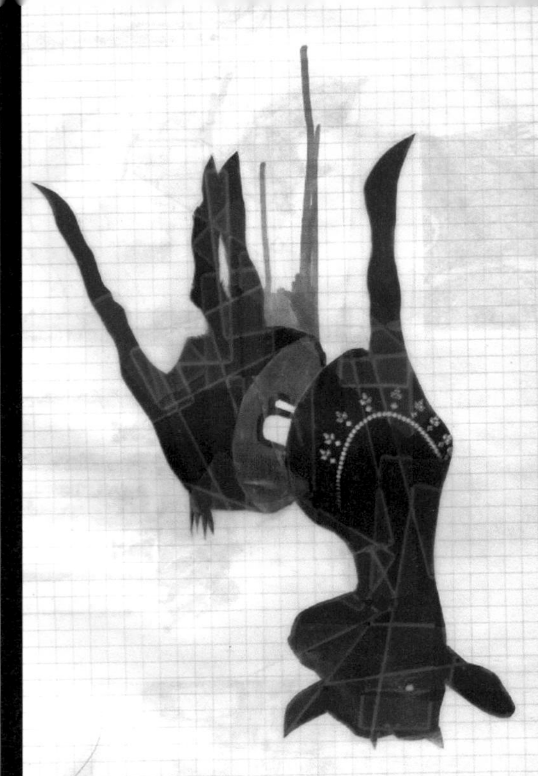

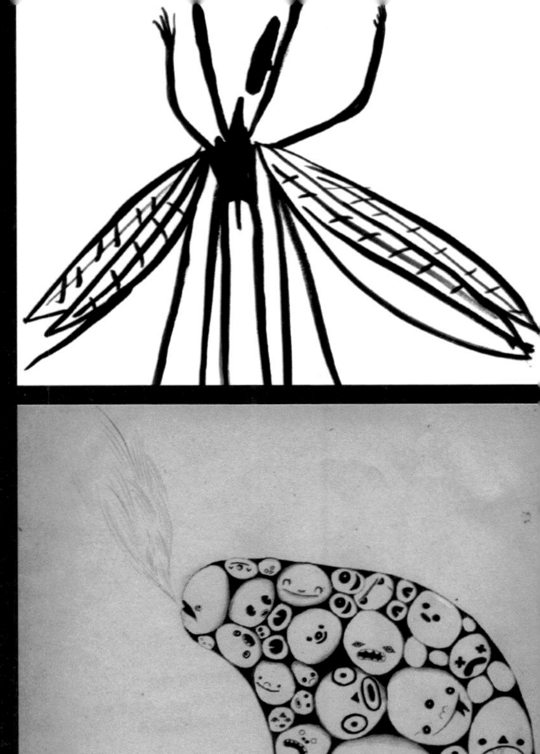

SAMOS

SPECIAL FORCES
CLOUD CITY
CLOUD CITY
CLOUD CITY
IN STORES DEC. 20TH
IN STORES 12/6

FriendsWithYou
FRIENDS
WITH
MALFI IS
YOUR

Illusions
CARNE

BUS
K
Diplomat Mall
I HIT
GARY
IN THE
THIGH

Thank you:

There is absolutely too many of you that we love and have helped us greatly on this journey, if for some reason you are not in this list, you are still in our hearts . Thank you all for helping us spread our magic, love, and joy all over the world.

A special thanks goes to both of our families for molding us into who we are.
All of our Grandparents: Sosa, Cirita, Arturo, Herman and Rozzy Barnett, and a special thanks to Grammy, and Nana, Papa the Barnetts, Kapis and the Harrisons. Our parents Elliot, Raysy, Jane, and Mindy, Arturo Sr. & Marianela... Our brothers and sisters: Emy & Ryan Stark and her new baby, Min, Marla Michelle, Lacy Rose, Leonel, Paloma, and Palomita. • and Sweet little Jackie Valle
A warm thanks to my wife Melody, and my daughter Lola Sol Sandoval. • Thank you DGV, Robert, Henni, Jannie, Lina, Vinzenz and the rest of the crew. • STRANGECO and its crew: Jimmy, Emy, Tiger, and Greg • I love Dust and its crew: Mark, Dan and Alex • Our own faithfully crew of brothers who are always there to help us: Yamile and Golden eyes, Azulito, Andres, Sebastian, Leo, Maria, Louisa, PJ Mark, and our own Mr. Christopher Lee Boon. • Our friends Alvaro (*our buddy and Miami pics), Mike D, Press (*sweet miami baby and squid pics with Harlan), Manny, Jessie Ray & Cindy, Cookieheadz Alex Caso, David "Suede" Gonzalez, Hanna Fushihara!, Jesus, and the Jews, Jorgy Bear, Kim and Jessica. Martha, Manny, Otto Van Shirach, Yago, Schafer, Bruuuutha, Adam and Ryan, David Haxton, Rich our spiritual brother, Dan Nadel, Paperrrrraaaaaadddd, Mickey Mouse, Grimace, Anpan Man, and Domo Kun, Astro Boy and Buddha, Black & White, Brad Birdie Britton, The Harrisons, Mumbleboy, David Choe and his posse, Harry, Joe Toe, Gary Baseman, Mark Ryden, Tim Biskup, Boris Hoppek, Julian Pablo Manzelli, Doma, Orilo, Walter, Diego, Navas, Lum, Pepe, Locomotion and all it people! Maddie, Frookie, Miyazaki, Jodorowsky, Tezuka, Peter Thaler, Lars and the Pictoplasma crew. Dicken Schrader and BEBE Chaguire, Kidrobot and its crew, Paul, Chad, Nicole • MOCA, Bonnie Clearwater, Giant Robot. Brenty, and Eric, Nina Arias, Jose Diaz, Mariano Dabini, Drew Stoddard, Silvia (Yogi Master) MAlfi and all the spirits that guide us. Merry Karnowsky and Akiko. Swindle: Roger and Sonja and Caleb, J Jamie O'Shea, Rolan Vega, The Handsome Panther aka Jon Garin, and Naomi, Nick D Lobo, SCHEMATIC Josh , Melanie, and Rom, JUICY PANIC, Tropical Restaurant, to all of our fans, magazines and everyone who has helped us along the way...

The light and the love
SAM & TURY!

All works depicted in this book are created and the sole property of Samuel Albert Borkson and Arturo Sandoval III with the exception of the contributors listed below... Photographed by Sebastian Grey: p. 4, 6, 8,10-12, 22-24, 92-95, 117, 122, 128-133 • Photographed by Tiger Corpora: p. 5, 8-9, 11 • Photographed by Kyle Baker: p. 22-23, 25 p. 71: Rainbow & Cloudy monster illustration done in collaboration with Mike del Marmol (Typestereo.com), Alvaro Ilizarbe (freegums.com) & Pres Rodriguez. • p. 73: Illustration done in collaboration with NOAH, visit safeskittens.com • p. 77: Illustration done in collaboration with Mumble Boy (mumbleboy.com) and Julian Gatto (gagainc.com) • p. 80-81: Illustration done by Jemma Hostetler of Pirate™ Computer Channel. • p. 98-99, 122: Sculpting and molding by Azul Cadenas. • p. 106-107: (The Birth of the Fox: Meet Albino Fox; Installation at Autostadt Wolfsburg, 2006), courtesy of galerie heliumcowboy artspace • p. 110-111: Mural painting by David Choe. • p. 117: Photography by Sara Padgett (home-tapes.com) p. 138-139: Photography by Jennifer Stark & Alvaro Ilizarbe.

FRIENDSWITHYOU HAVE POWERS!
by Sam Borkson & Arturo Sandoval

Edited by Robert Klanten & Hendrik Hellige
Project Management & Layout : Hendrik Hellige / dgv • Production Management: Vinzenz Geppert / dgv
Foreword: Sonja Commentz • Captions: Lina Kunimoto / dgv

Printed by Graphicom, Italy

Published by Die Gestalten Verlag, Berlin 2006
ISBN 10: 3-89955-163-X – ISBN 13: 978-3-89955-163-1

Bibliographic information published by Die Deutsche Bibliothek. The Deutsche Bibliothek lists this publication in the Deutsche Nationalbibliografie; detailed bibliographic data is available on the Internet at http://dnb.ddb.de.

For more information please check: www.die-gestalten.de

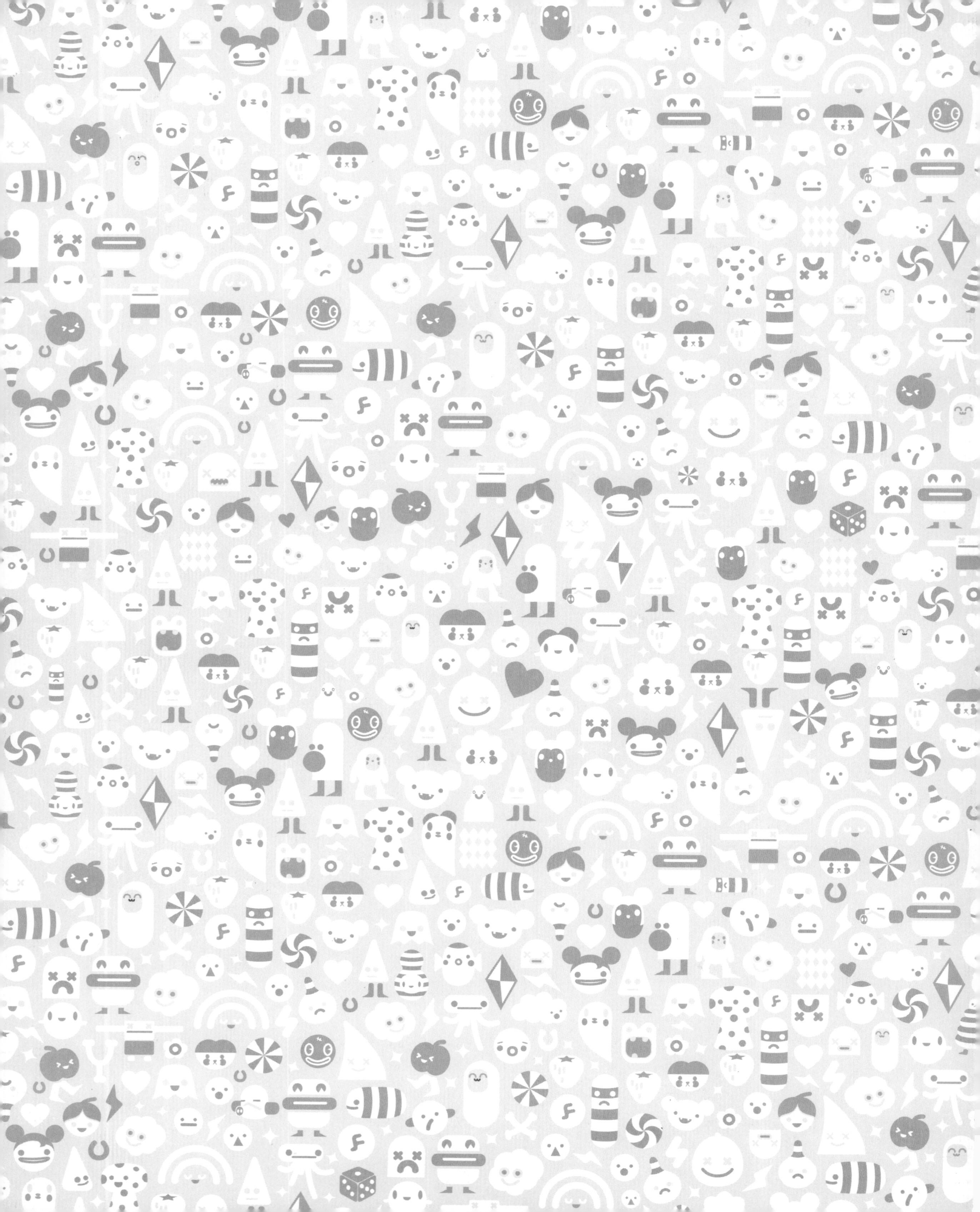